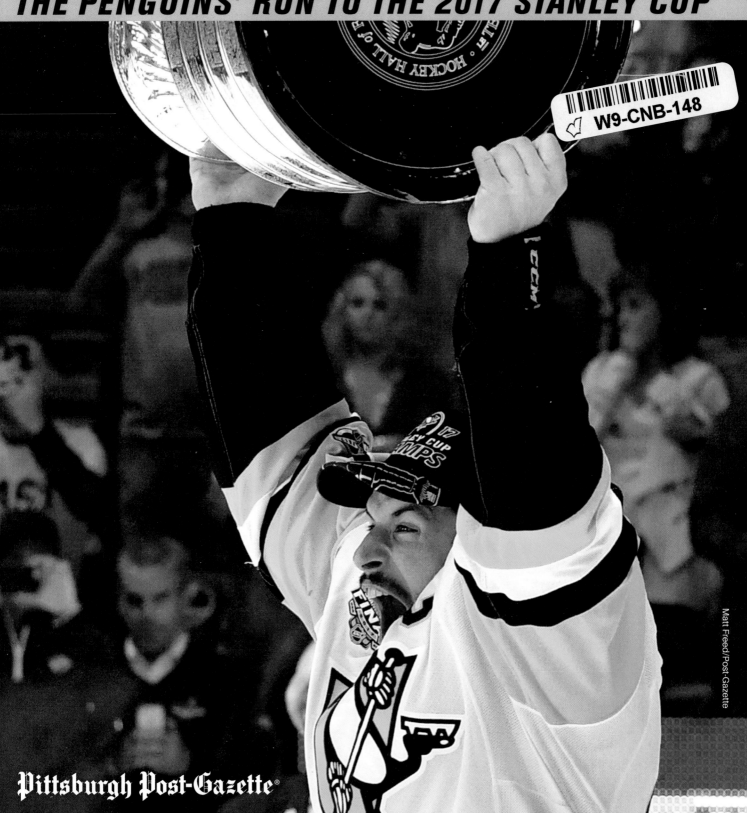

SPECIAL COMMEMORATIVE BOOK

STANLEY'S SEQUEL

THE PENGUINS' RUN TO THE 2017 STANLEY CUP

W9-CNB-148

Pittsburgh Post-Gazette®

This book is available in quantity at special discounts for your group or organization. For further information, contact:

Triumph Books LLC
814 North Franklin Street
Chicago, Illinois 60610
Phone: (312) 337-0747
www.triumphbooks.com

Printed in U.S.A.
ISBN: 978-1-62937-356-0

Pittsburgh Post-Gazette
John Robinson Block, Co-publisher and Editor-in-Chief
David M. Shribman, Executive Editor and Vice-President
Susan L. Smith, Managing Editor
Jim Iovino, Deputy Managing Editor

BOOK EDITORS
Michael Sanserino, Assistant Managing Editor, Sports
Tyler Batiste, Sports Editor
Alex Iniguez, Associate Sports Editor

PHOTO EDITORS
Sally Stapleton and Melissa Tkach

ADMINISTRATIVE COORDINATOR
Allison Latcheran, Senior Marketing Manager

Content packaged by Mojo Media, Inc.
Jason Hinman: Creative Director
Joe Funk: Editor

Front cover photo by AP Images
Back cover photo by Matt Freed/Post-Gazette

contents

Introduction

By David M. Shribman

Not since Ernest Hemingway wrote about a single marlin off the Florida coast has one fish — a junk fish, if we here in Pittsburgh are perfectly honest about it, with 16 grams of protein and 12 grams of fat composing, as the local gendarmes put it in an unfortunate but unforgettable phrase, one "instrument of crime" — won so much notoriety. Not since the original rules of British football were written in 1863 has a single offside meant so much.

Not since, well, last year, have the Pittsburgh Penguins staged a victory parade, held Lord Stanley's Cup on high, and booked boozy bacchanalias from Regina, Saskatchewan, to Boden, Sweden.

Here we go again. Jason Miller won a Pulitzer Prize in 1972 for a play set in Pennsylvania called *That Champion Season.* In those 45 years Pittsburgh has lived a drama *called Those Championship Seasons* — six from the Steelers, one from the Pirates, and now five from the Penguins. A dazzling dozen. Eat your heart out, Cleveland. Eat your catfish, Nashville. Pour on a half-cup of buttermilk and be generous with that onion powder.

But there was something special about this championship season. A stellar year from Sidney Crosby. Shimmery performances from Evgeni Malkin. Another gritty round from Matt Murray. And — lest we forget — a victory tour and valedictory performance from Marc-Andre Fleury, a flower worthy of Whitman: *When lilacs last in the dooryard bloom'd,/ And the great star early droop'd in the western sky in the night.*

The rest of the team was, if you will pardon the expression, poetry in motion, though more an epic verse than a haiku, requiring repeated seventh games to get to the top spot. No one in these precincts seemed to complain; yes, those extra games were irritating—and any more than four games was deemed unnecessary by the local lords—but those extra contests merely served to extend a season splashed with stardust. Even those few beyond the gravitational pull of the winter game benefited. There were no lines at the Giant Eagle after 8 p.m. on game nights.

And yet one line of an entirely different sort — *Love is lovelier the second time around* — seemed to be the soundtrack of our town, for this Stanley Cup, won, as the great sports commentator Frank Sinatra might have said, with both *feet on the ground,* seemed just as sweet, maybe even sweeter, than last year's.

The Pittsburgh Penguins celebrate after winning their second straight Stanley Cup. (Peter Diana/Post-Gazette)

All of Pittsburgh was schooled in the unlikelihood of a Cup repeat, all those statistics and precedents pouring over the airwaves and across vast acreage of print, but wasn't it our very own Sphenisciformes who won consecutive Stanley Cups in 1991 and 1992? Didn't our flightless birds already perform this trick?

Of course they did. But it was different this time.

It wasn't that the Pens had a sense of entitlement; no one who watched that Washington Capitals team roar into town flecked with destiny could possibly have felt this. It wasn't that the Pens had a patina of inevitability; no one who witnessed the feats of the Ottawa Senators could possibly have believed that.

And the Predators? From a town with annual average snowfall of 7 inches and average January temperature of 37 degrees, they were at first blush hard to take seriously here in our wintry redoubt. They had, to be sure, the Grand Ole Opry and the Country Music Hall of Fame, the Johnny Cash Museum and, if you are history-minded, the Hermitage home of Donald J. Trump's favorite president, Andrew Jackson. But hockey? A transplant sport with shallow roots. Indeed, their entire fanbase has been serving a bench minor for years.

That last round — the Stanley Cup Final — was not so much a hockey game as a clash of cultures, a match of yin and yang.

They eat fried chicken at Monell's, or hot chicken at Hattie B's. We eat fried fish sandwiches at Wholey's or at Nied's Hotel. They root for a baseball team called the Nashville Sounds, which plays in the Pacific Coast League. We root for a baseball team that actually is in the major leagues. They eat cornmeal pancakes. We eat whatever Pamela serves us. They sit on one river. It is well known how many we sit on.

Our superiority was on display for all the world to see, though it might have been better had no one witnessed that second period of the first game. In opening shots our town looked splendid and shiny, office towers and yellow bridges against a darkening sky — a scene hard to resist and, as the denizens of Nashville discovered, hard to beat. But everything about our hockey holiday of 2017 was hard to beat.

And so in the pages that follow we relive this championship season, played to a vintage soundtrack, featuring a song first performed in the film "High Town" with orchestration by Henry Mancini, a graduate of Aliquippa High, and ending in music, as this season of sparkle and spectacle did, with this lyrical reflection on love, the second time around:

Who can say what brought us to this miracle we've found?

There are those who'll bet love comes but once, and yet

I'm oh, so glad we met the second time around

David M. Shribman is executive editor of the Pittsburgh Post-Gazette. His family's greatest distinction is that his grandfather was evicted from the Montreal Forum for spitting in the face of a rival fan.

The final buzzer sounds at the end of the Penguins' Cup-clinching Game 6 victory in Nashville. (Peter Diana/Post-Gazette)

MAY 29, 2017 · PITTSBURGH, PENNSYLVANIA
PENGUINS 5, PREDATORS 3

Early Wake-Up Call
Guentzel Nets Winner After Lead Evaporates
By Jason Mackey

They were the first words out of Penguins coach Mike Sullivan's mouth late Monday.

He could've quit right there, honestly. Pretty much hit the nail on the head, even if his team couldn't hit the net with a puck for much of this one.

"We weren't very good," Sullivan said. "You know, we weren't very good."

It's tough to argue. The Penguins were lousy and fortunate to leave PPG Paints Arena with a 5-3 win over the Nashville Predators in Game 1 of the Stanley Cup final.

Somehow.

Despite blowing a three-goal lead.

Forget dictating terms. Despite failing to register a shot on goal for a stretch of exactly 37 minutes that bridged all three periods and accounted for more than 60 percent of the entire game.

"This team usually, for the most part, is pretty good at making sure that we're continuing to play the game the right way," Sullivan said. "Tonight, that wasn't the case. We just weren't very good."

Before getting too specific, Jake Guentzel bailed the Penguins out with what turned out to be the game-winning goal at 16:43 of the third period. Nick Bonino tacked on an empty-netter.

The Penguins lead the series, 1-0, with Game 2 back here on Wednesday. The winner of Game 1 has won the Stanley Cup 78 percent of the time.

Nearly falling into an early series hole can be attributed to a few primary factors:

- The Penguins lost the special teams battle. Nashville went 2 for 3 on the power play, the same unit that converted that many times on 22 chances last round. After allowing just one power-play goal against Ottawa, Ryan Ellis and Colton Sissons made the Penguins pay.
- Nashville's defense did something drastically different than what the Penguins saw from the Senators: They played aggressive. It forced the Penguins forwards to make quick decisions with the puck, and that did not end well.

"Their D played pretty much in your face," Bonino said. "They make you dump the puck poorly. When you do, [goaltender Pekka] Rinne plays it really well. It's tough to establish a forecheck like that. It's tough to get odd-man rushes like that."

Predators left winger Filip Forsberg tumbles over Penguins goalie Matt Murray during Game 1 of the Stanley Cup final at PPG Paints Arena. (Peter Diana/Post-Gazette)

Or, evidently, shots on goal.

Get this: The Penguins only attempted 11 shots in the first, six in the second and 11 more in the third.

According to Penguins historian Bob Grove, their 12 shots on goal were the Penguins' fewest ever in a playoff game.

"I think they out-played us for most of the night," Justin Schultz said. "We can't expect to win if we play like that."

• Winning like this might also bring about questions of whether the Penguins are tired. Nobody has played more hockey since the start of last season. Nashville (six) had twice as many days off before this one.

Olli Maatta didn't want to hear about fatigue being an excuse.

"It shouldn't be," he said.

Still, Nashville was clearly the more energetic team.

"We talked a lot about our compete level," Maatta said. "We didn't bring it today."

• Guentzel's goal could be a template. Matt Cullen made a smart chip play off the wall, allowing Guentzel to enter the offensive zone with speed.

When the Penguins are humming, that's what they do. It didn't happen, however, for enough of Monday's game.

The Penguins will also look to eliminate the number of stretch passes they used in this one.

"That's our game — playing fast," Schultz said

of the last goal. "When we're doing it, we're creating stuff. We didn't use our speed. Our defensemen weren't moving it up quick enough or joining the attack. It's everyone. We have to be better."

A disallowed goal at 7:13 of the first period swung the momentum in the Penguins' favor, as officials ruled Filip Forsberg was offside after a Sullivan challenge.

That triggered a run of goals by Evgeni Malkin, Conor Sheary and Bonino in a stretch of 4:11, but that's when the shots on goal stopped coming.

"We were yelling at everyone to shoot the puck," Sheary recalled. "Rinne hadn't seen one in a while. Maybe would catch him by surprise."

Ellis scored midway through the second, and Sissons and Frederick Gaudreau tied it in the third before the Penguins woke up.

"You never think you're going to blow a three-goal lead," Bonino said. "When we did, we almost knew it was coming. It wasn't like it snuck up on us. We knew they were coming. We weren't playing well. It woke us up a bit, then Jake saved us there. Times like that you just have to keep playing hard, stay focused, and it worked out for us."

The challenge for the Penguins will be internalizing what went wrong in this one, correcting the mistakes at practice and avoiding a repeat performance.

"We trust the leadership of the group that we have, that they get it," Sullivan said. "They understand. They know we weren't at our best. We had that discussion after the game.

"This is something we'll learn from and we'll try to make sure that we respond the right way for Game 2." ■

Sidney Crosby celebrates after Evgeni Malkin scores in the first period against the Predators. (Peter Diana/PostGazette)

Stanley Cup Final, Game 2

MAY 31, 2017 · PITTSBURGH, PENNSYLVANIA
PENGUINS 4, PREDATORS 1

Rookie Revelation

Guentzel Stars Again as Penguins Chase Rinne From Game 2

By Jason Mackey

From the moment he reached the NHL, Jake Guentzel has been off to the races. First game, first shift, first shot, first goal. Two total in his NHL debut. Stealing the spotlight in the Penguins' Stadium Series game. Then nine goals in Guentzel's first 11 playoff games.

After a slight lag, look out: Penguins coach Mike Sullivan believes his rookie scorer may have gotten a second wind. As a result, Guentzel could be in line to pick up some major hardware.

Guentzel scored a pair of goals Wednesday in Game 2 of the Stanley Cup final to ignite a 4-1 Penguins victory against the Nashville Predators at PPG Paints Arena, giving him an NHL-high 12 so far this postseason.

"He's amazing," Evgeni Malkin said of Guentzel, the favorite for the Conn Smythe Trophy should the Penguins close this out.

How we got here, though, is truly the amazing part.

On Sunday, Guentzel looked like a healthy scratch. He took one line rush during practice while rotating on a fourth line with Carl Hagelin, Matt Cullen and Patric Hornqvist, who was set to return from an upper-body injury.

By Monday's Game 1, Guentzel was a cute little story. In the lineup after all, the well-liked, soft-spoken Guentzel scored the game-winning goal.

After Game 2, Guentzel became the story league-wide.

"He's mature, but he wants to go to those tough areas," Chris Kunitz said. "He wants to score those big goals. He has the skill set to create things on his own, but he also has the knack to put pucks on the net. I think when you have that fearless attitude, you have a chance to get pucks that get closer to you when you go to those tough areas. He's done a great job of scoring big goals for our team."

In 21 postseason games, Guentzel has 12 goals and 19 points, most ever for an American-born rookie. He's two goals shy of Dino Ciccarelli's rookie record from 1980-81. Five of Guentzel's goals have been game-winners.

According to Penguins historian Bob Grove, that's more than every other Penguins rookie since the start of the 2000 postseason combined.

"He brings energy," Matt Cullen said of Guentzel, who's 18 years younger than Cullen. "He's hanging onto pucks. He's making plays.

Jake Guentzel scores on Pekka Rinne in the third period of Game 2, another stunning playoff performance from the Penguins rookie. (Matt Freed/Post-Gazette)

"Obviously he's finishing so well right now, but he does everything. He puts himself in good spots to score goals."

Late in the Eastern Conference semifinals, Sullivan worried Guentzel might be wearing down, the result of his smaller frame and never having handled the rigors of an NHL schedule.

So Sullivan and his staff made a concerted effort to cut Guentzel's minutes. Less is more, they figured. Guentzel has rewarded the coaching staff by bouncing back in a big way.

"He was great," Sullivan said of a few one-on-one conversations he had with Guentzel during an eight-game goal-less stretch. "He's a conscientious kid. He's a pleasure to coach. We just talked about playing the game the right way.

"He's a real talented kid. We just tried to shift the focus a little bit with him. We tried to cut his minutes because he was playing a lot of minutes.

"I think he's had an opportunity to get a little bit of a second wind. He's getting his legs back. I think his confidence is there."

Guentzel scored the Penguins' first goal at 16:36 of the first period, finishing the rebound of a Conor Sheary shot from in tight. He notched the game-winner at 10 seconds of the third period, off a juicy rebound courtesy of Nashville goaltender Pekka Rinne.

"We've been talking about putting pucks off pads," Guentzel said. "It happens. Great pass."

Great effort overall from the Penguins, one that puts them in the driver's seat in this series.

Figure that 45 of the 50 teams that have jumped out to a 2-0 lead in the Stanley Cup final have gone on to win the series, a 90-percent success rate.

Scott Wilson and Malkin scored 15 seconds apart in the third period to turn this into a quasi-laugher, while Matt Murray stopped 37 of 38 shots to deliver yet another dominant performance at home.

It's appropriate those three had a hand in the win.

Wilson is one of Guentzel's good friends. Malkin was the Penguins' Conn Smythe winner in 2009, and Murray was the precocious, unflappable rookie a season ago.

"He's a good kid off the ice, so he's fun to be around," Wilson said. "That never changed when he wasn't getting the bounces."

Sort of like Murray. No matter the shot, the period, the day of the week or what he had for breakfast, Murray focuses on one thing: stopping the puck.

Only for Guentzel, it's scoring goals, not preventing them.

"He's a confident kid," Murray said. "He really wanted to break that slump he was in. He's done it in a big way for us. Just like he was all season long and all playoffs long. He's a motivated kid. It doesn't surprise me at all to see him get two. He's been huge for us." ■

Penguins teammates line up for the national anthem before taking on the Predators at PPG Paints Arena. (Matt Freed/Post-Gazette)

JUNE 3, 2017 · NASHVILLE, TENNESSEE
PREDATORS 5, PENGUINS 1

Southern Discomfort

Power Play Struggles as Predators Grab Game 3

By Jason Mackey

Nobody could have reasonably expected the Nashville Predators to fade quietly into the night.

They don't do anything below maximum decibel level. Why on Earth wouldn't they crank it up for the first Stanley Cup final game in Music City?

The Predators' 5-1 win over the Penguins in Game 3 Saturday included many ingredients, but any sort of postgame analysis should start with a caveat: Hey, the Predators don't stink.

Predators goalie Pekka Rinne makes save on the Penguins' Carter Rowney Saturday in Game 3 of the Stanley Cup final at Bridgestone Arena.

"It's a seven-game series," Penguins coach Mike Sullivan said. "It's a long series. We knew this was going to be a hard-fought battle. That's exactly what it is.

"We've got to try and respond the right way."

The Predators had won seven of eight games at Bridgestone Arena in these playoffs. They swept the Chicago Blackhawks and beat the St. Louis Blues and Anaheim Ducks in six games to get here, locking down those teams' respective stars en route to victory.

Back home in front of their hockey-mad fans, a city that has been whipped into a frenzy by how cool playoff hockey can be whenever it's hot outside, the Predators turned this thing into a series

again with a superb performance on home ice.

"They were the more desperate team," captain Sidney Crosby said. "That was pretty evident."

Instead of using a collection of highly skilled players to gain momentum, the Penguins are losing it when this group takes the ice.

"It's not working," Evgeni Malkin said. "We need to change something, maybe players, I don't know. It's tough to say right now. I know we can play better on the power play."

Worse, the key cogs on the Penguins power play — Sidney Crosby, Malkin and Phil Kessel — finished with three shots on goal and eight shot attempts on Saturday.

Crosby talked about the same stuff. It was a combined of missing the net and Predators shot blocks. Sullivan said postgame the Penguins are still trying to get Kessel to have more of a shoot-first attitude, and there's increasing speculation that he's not exactly healthy.

Meanwhile, Nashville's power play struck for a key goal early in the second period, which kick-started a three-goal run and gave the Predators confidence. Mattias Ekholm added a second man-advantage marker late.

"They got some momentum when they got that power play goal," Crosby said of Roman Josi's score at 5:51 of the second period.

Playing from behind, the Penguins were also

Sidney Crosby battles Predators defenseman P.K. Subban for the puck in what was a disappointing Game 3 showing for the visiting Penguins. (Peter Diana/Post-Gazette)

forced to take a bunch of chances and, as a result, coughed up a few odd-man rushes.

The most obvious might have been a neutral-zone turnover by Chris Kunitz in the third period that led to a breakaway goal for Craig Smith. Not all Kunitz's fault. The puck hit Kessel's skate. But it still resulted in a chance the other way.

The Predators seemed to target Matt Murray's glove hand and scored three times that way. Murray said afterward he was happy with his positioning on the goals; it simply came down to making the save.

"I thought I was in the right spot on almost all of them," Murray said. "A couple weird bounces. … It's just about making a save."

One good element for the Penguins was play of Carl Hagelin, Matt Cullen and Patric Hornqvist.

They strung together several solid shifts early, but the group was unable to beat Rinne.

The Penguins were beaten by a team Saturday that simply wanted it more.

While that hasn't happened a ton under Sullivan — it's the first time they've suffered back-to-back road losses in the postseason on his watch — it's not exactly revolutionary for the opposing team to have a bounce-back game at home.

Its players get paid, too.

"They were hungrier," Malkin said. "We played [well] the first period, then we gave them so much space; they controlled the puck. We lost control after first period. We took a couple penalties and gave them a couple breakaways. It's not our game.

"We need to forget that, look forward and look to next game." ■

JUNE 5, 2017 · NASHVILLE, TENNESSEE
PREDATORS 4, PENGUINS 1

Tennessee Two-Step

Predators Change Tone with Back-to-Back Wins

By Jason Mackey

Less than a week ago the Penguins flew to Nashville holding a 2-0 series lead and were brimming with confidence. Back then, Predators goaltender Pekka Rinne couldn't stop a beach ball. The Penguins' offense was clicking. The thought of a sweep was plausible.

Times have certainly changed.

If the Penguins' 4-1 loss to Nashville in Game 4 of the Stanley Cup final Monday at Bridgestone Arena told us anything, it's that these final three games should be a lot of fun.

"We've been on both sides of it here," Penguins coach Mike Sullivan said. "Both teams have won two games. These games are a lot closer than the score indicates. I think that was the case in our building. I think it was the case in this building. We've got to stay with it."

How much flipped with a trip to Music City?

When the Penguins flew south, Rinne's save percentage was already there to greet them — .778. The past two games, he's stood on his head, allowing just two goals.

"He's a great goaltender," Guentzel said of Rinne, who stopped 23 of 24 Monday and 50 of 52 over the two games here. "He can make those kinds of saves. I have to do a better job putting them in the back of the net."

We also saw two offensive talents for the Predators shine bright, one maybe you've heard about, another who doesn't even have his own dressing room stall.

The first, Viktor Arvidsson scored for the first time since Game 4 of the Western Conference final and may have busted out of a prolonged slump; he looked like the guy who tied for the Predators' regular season lead in goals with 31.

Rookie Frederick Gaudreau — who sits on a folding chair to change out of his hockey equipment — scored his third goal of the series, as he's quickly become Nashville's answer to Guentzel.

The Penguins had more shot attempts (57-50) and enjoyed a boatload of Grade-A opportunities. Furthermore, 21 of those attempts came from Sidney Crosby, Evgeni Malkin and Phil Kessel.

The near misses included Guentzel from point-blank range off a Crosby feed at 2:31 of the second. Then a breakaway for Chris Kunitz at 3:29. In the first, Bryan Rust shot wide, and Guentzel had another on the doorstep. The Penguins even — don't fall over — flashed some flow on the power play.

No dice.

Instead, Gaudreau scored on a wrap-around to make it 2-1 at 3:45 of the second after officials went back to look at video that showed the puck crossing the goal line.

Sidney Crosby scores the Penguins' lone goal of Game 4 at Bridgestone Arena in Nashville. (Peter Diana/Post-Gazette)

Crosby started a three-second sequence with a mini-breakaway, tried to stuff a rebound, and Rinne went all Flying Wallenda to rob Guentzel.

Still nothing. Except, of course, when Arvidsson broke free and beat Murray glove side.

"I thought tonight we generated some really good chances," Crosby said. "It just comes down to burying your chances. They got a couple and buried them. We didn't."

The good part for the Penguins is they have plenty of experience not panicking.

Overall, several Penguins players thought this was their best team game of the series. The only problem was the result didn't match.

"We definitely found a different level [Monday]," Crosby said. "Didn't get the result we wanted. If we can continue to get those chances, they'll go in for us."

Fixing how the Penguins defended a few goals will be a focal point. It wasn't great all-around, and Sullivan was pretty overt about that.

But he also expressed confidence in his group that it will be able to make those corrections before Game 5.

"I thought in both games there were a couple that I think we could done a better job defending with awareness away from the puck that could have been prevented," Sullivan said.

"But we believe in this group we have. They're a resilient bunch. They're a resourceful bunch. They understand how to win. We just have to go back home, and we've got to respond the right way." ◾

Stanley Cup Final, Game 5

JUNE 8, 2017 · PITTSBURGH, PENNSYLVANIA
PENGUINS 6, PREDATORS 0

Flying High

Crosby Shines as Penguins Pull Within One Game of the Cup
By Jason Mackey

It took 50 seconds Thursday to see that the Penguins and captain Sidney Crosby meant business. That's when Crosby sliced through a pair of Predators defenders and drew a holding call on Ryan Ellis.

The final 59:10 turned out to be a mere affirmation of what we saw then, and probably what we should have seen all along: The Penguins, their 2016-17 eulogy being penned by some, responded in resounding fashion.

By key players. In important elements of the game. All over the joint, really, as the Penguins' 6-0 win against the Predators in Game 5 of the Stanley Cup final Thursday at PPG Paints Arena put them one win away from the franchise's fifth Stanley Cup.

One that would bring with it some serious historical significance, too; if the Penguins can win Game 6 Sunday at Bridgestone Arena in Nashville, they'll become the first repeat Cup winners since the Red Wings in 1997-98.

"This team has a certain businesslike approach to it," Penguins coach Mike Sullivan said. "It starts with our veteran players and our leadership group. These guys, they just get it. They understand the importance of response games and making sure that we have the right mindset going into these types of games."

Leading the charge there were Crosby and Evgeni Malkin, the franchise centers, the guys who combined for zero shots on goal during Game 3.

In Game 4, however, the Penguins flipped the script. Offense and scoring chances came. Only the goals lacked.

They got a tangible reward Thursday.

"I think we turned the page," Crosby said. "Looking at that game, we felt like we still generated some good chances.

"I think we felt like if we did a few things differently but buried those chances we'd give ourselves a chance to win. We did that, especially early on."

Such as when Justin Schultz, Bryan Rust and Malkin scored first-period goals, the one from Schultz coming on the power play.

Talk about a response. There was plenty

Sidney Crosby withstands checks from Predators Matt Irwin and Yannick Weber during the Penguins' dominant Game 5 win in Pittsburgh. (Peter Diana/Post-Gazette)

of chatter about the power play. It joined the defensemen, Sullivan's line combinations, Phil Kessel's scoring touch and who to start in goal as the freak-out topics of Penguins fans as Game 5 neared — thankful aren't we all for the drawn-out schedule.

"Finally [a] power play score," Malkin would say afterward.

And finally Kessel scored, too, another source of some ridicule and panic.

He whipped a shot from the high slot past Juuse Saros, who came on in relief of Pekka Rinne, who again was awful in Pittsburgh.

Kessel's goal and the Penguins' win backed up Malkin's post-practice prediction from Wednesday.

"If we [don't] score, you guys kill me," Malkin teased. "It's not just me and Phil. The whole team did a great job tonight. It's an unbelievable win."

Remember that whole goalie freak-out? Matt Murray again made Sullivan look like a smart man — not that doing so is all that hard at this point — by turning aside all 24 shots he faced.

A response game from Murray, who allowed eight goals in Games 3-4, even if he wasn't in the mood to revel in it.

"Of course you want to win every game," Murray said. "So, sure, you want a good bounce-back game after a bad one, but at the end of the day, you just prepare the same way each and every day and try to give yourself the best chance to be successful.

"I'm definitely a competitive guy, but I try to take things one step at a time and not get too far ahead of myself."

Also remember worrying about what to do with Conor Sheary? Or if he should play at all?

Bounced to the press box earlier these playoffs, Sheary found himself reunited with Crosby and scored the Penguins' fourth goal.

Similarly, Ron Hainsey tossed his hand into the pile. Among the group of ridiculed defensemen after that non-productive trip to Nashville, all Hainsey did was score a goal, add an assist and deliver two crucial hits, one on Calle Jarnkrok in the corner on an early penalty kill.

As a group, the Penguins defensemen were much more efficient and responsible on breakouts, and the team, as a whole, flashed a ton of physicality.

But don't stray too much from the source on this one. The effort the Penguins fed off of the most came from the guy with jump from the jump — Crosby.

"You knew he had the jump right in the early game there," Guentzel said.

"He's our leader," Murray said, "so everybody kind of follows what he does." ■

Chris Kunitz fights the Predators' Yannick Weber in the third period of Game 5. (Matt Freed/Post-Gazette)

the course of the year. I really believe that the resilience of this team has become a strength."

Sunday marked the 213rd game the Penguins have played since the start of the 2015-16 regular season. Nobody has played more hockey, and that's without taking into account the World Cup of Hockey.

"We're tired," Evgeni Malkin said. "But tomorrow we'll wake up, and it's a new day, an amazing day. Great summer, for sure."

Sullivan became the second coach in NHL history to win back-to-back Stanley Cup titles in his first two seasons with a team. Toe Blake was the only other coach to do it, in 1957.

Crosby became the first back-to-back winner of the Conn Smythe since Penguins co-owner Mario Lemieux in 1991 and 1992.

Postgame, Crosby's handoff of the Cup was to Ron Hainsey, who had never before played a playoff game. Next came Matt Cullen, who might have played his last game in the NHL, and fellow veteran Chris Kunitz.

"It was great," Hainsey said. "I was kind of voting for a couple other guys. Kunitz or Cullen, who it might be his last game. But it was a great honor."

Game 6 came down to the wire. Patric Hornqvist smacked the rebound of a Justin Schultz shot off Pekka Rinne's elbow at 18:25 of the third period.

The goal withstood a challenge from Nashville coach Peter Laviolette for goaltender interference before another of the Penguins' Swedes, Carl Hagelin, added an empty-net goal with 13.6 seconds left.

"It feels great," Hornqvist said. "There's been a lot of guys telling us we can't do it, and now

Evgeni Malkin (left) kisses the Stanley Cup and Sidney Crosby shares in the celebration following the Penguins' thrilling Game 6 win in Nashville. (Matt Freed/Post-Gazette)

we're standing here. We're going to celebrate in Pittsburgh in a few days. This [win] says a lot about this team. We've battled through a lot."

Emotions were plenty high after the game. Cullen's voice crackled as he reflected on this journey and the thought that this might well have been his final NHL game.

"It's what it's all about," Cullen said. "I thank God every day for this. I just can't believe that it worked out this way, but I am so appreciative. It's just such a humbling experience. Never expected to have this opportunity. To have it work out like this, I'm really thankful."

Murray stopped all 27 shots he faced in yet another incredible playoff performance.

Afterward, he received the Cup from Marc-Andre Fleury, whose job Murray had taken. The young goaltender was blown away by the gesture.

"The fact that he handed me the Cup there says a lot about who Flower is," Murray said. "That meant so much to me for him to do that. I don't know what made him do that, but I'm very thankful for having him around, to call him a friend and a mentor. He's a special human being."

Fact is, the Penguins have a lot of special human beings on their team. Whether they're rookies such as Jake Guentzel, awestruck and soaking it all in, or Kunitz, who won his fourth Cup title, they're all special.

Otherwise they wouldn't be here, able to help write such a script. The same one their owner helped write a number of years ago.

"It's hard to win the Cup," Lemieux said. "To be able to win it back-to-back is special. It's something the people in this organization can cherish for the rest of our lives. It's unbelievable." ▪

Carl Hagelin celebrates on the ice after Game 6. Hagelin scored the Penguins' second goal on an empty-netter with 13.6 seconds left. (Matt Freed/ Post-Gazette)

Sidney Crosby Wins Conn Smythe Trophy for Second Consecutive Year

By Dave Molinari

Sidney Crosby didn't lead the Stanley Cup playoffs in scoring.

He had to settle for leading the Penguins to a championship.

Again.

Sure, Crosby was a major force in their offense — he finished the postseason with eight goals and 19 assists in 24 games, leaving him one point behind teammate Evgeni Malkin, the playoff leader — but not all of his contributions were tangible.

Heck, his most important ones probably weren't.

"You see it on the ice, but I think in talking with him and being around him, you can see a different level of drive and commitment," Penguins center Matt Cullen said recently. "I said this before early in the playoffs, in my short time with Sid I don't think I've ever seen him more committed, more determined."

For all he did, on and off the ice, to make the Penguins' fifth Stanley Cup possible, Crosby earned the Conn Smythe Trophy as playoff MVP for the second year in a row.

The Smythe winner was chosen in voting by a 15-member panel from the Professional Hockey Writers Association.

Crosby didn't get a Smythe ballot, but had a long list of worthy candidates if he'd been asked to vote.

"[Malkin] comes to mind right away," he said.

"I'd put our two goaltenders [Matt Murray and Marc-Andre Fleury] on there. There were games that they stole for us.

"[Jake Guentzel], for a guy to come in like that and score the way he did is pretty incredible. There are so many guys who could easily have won that."

Well, not really, for no player had an impact, during games or between them, rivaling Crosby's.

"He shows up on the scoresheet a lot, but it's not only that for our room," winger Conor Sheary said. "He does everything a leader should do, and he's proven that time in and time out.

"To see him get rewarded again with the Conn Smythe is pretty special."

Coincidentally enough, the last guy to win back-to-back Smythes also was a Penguins center. Fellow named Lemieux, who was on hand at Bridgestone Arena on Sunday night to watch the club he owns become the first team to win Cups in consecutive years since Detroit in 1997 and 1998.

The Penguins earned the first two of their five Cups when Lemieux was the cornerstone of franchise; the past three have come with Crosby filling that role.

Crosby isn't Lemieux's equal as a pure talent — face it, there are only a couple of candidates for that distinction — but he competes as ferociously as anyone who has played the game.

And it's contagious.

Sidney Crosby celebrates with Carl Hagelin after the final buzzer in Game 6 as the Penguins clinch their fifth Stanley Cup and second in as many years. (Peter Diana/Post-Gazette)

"He can propel your team, just by the way he plays the game," left winger Chris Kunitz said.

Crosby had one goal and six assists in six games during the final, but he made an indelible impression on his teammates long before that, as evidenced by winger Bryan Rust's assessment on the eve of Game 1 against Nashville.

"Sid's been kind of taking his game to a whole new level," Rust said. "He keeps rising to the occasion. He keeps getting better and better."

And now Crosby has a couple of Conn Smythe honors to prove that he's at his best when the games matter most.

He also seems motivated to do it again, based on his words while flanked by the Cup and the Smythe during a postgame press conference.

"You can't match this," Crosby said. "This is what it's all about." ◼

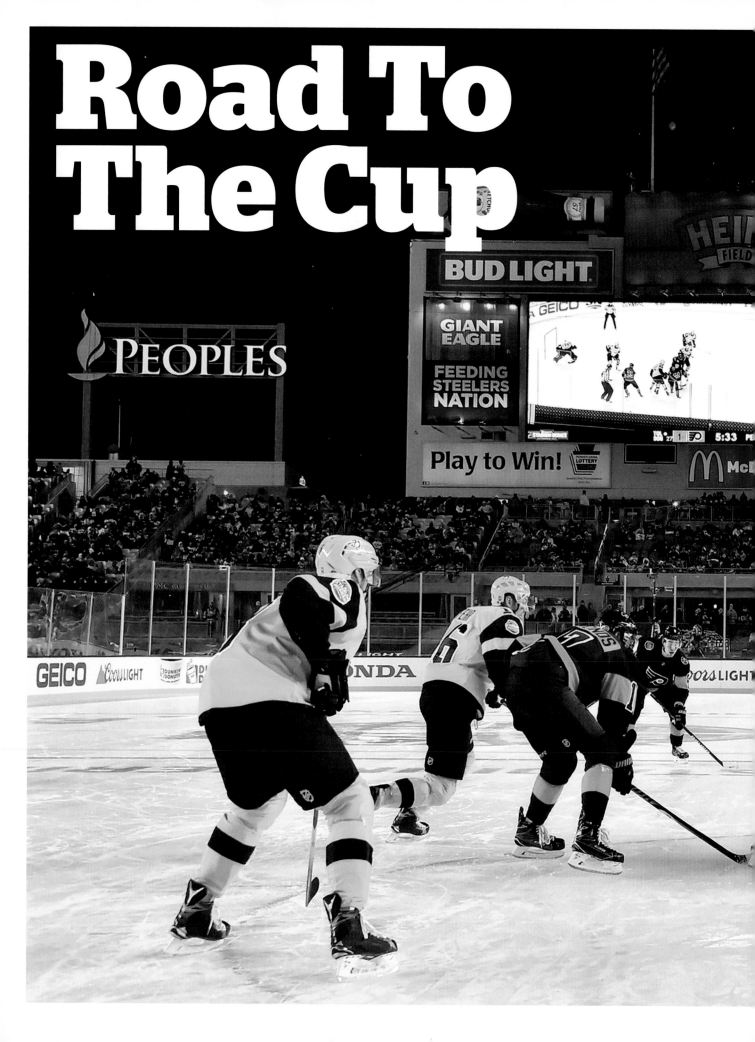

Road To The Cup

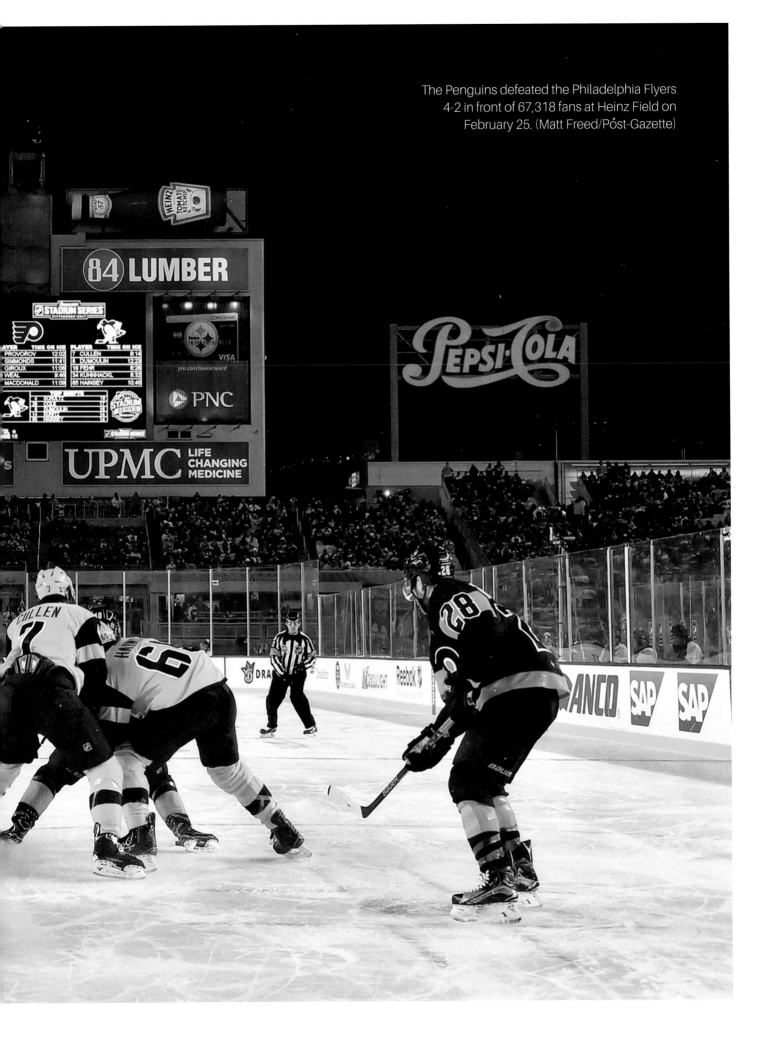

The Penguins defeated the Philadelphia Flyers 4-2 in front of 67,318 fans at Heinz Field on February 25. (Matt Freed/Post-Gazette)

The Quest to Win Again

Why Has it Become the Near-Impossible Dream?

By Dave Molinari • October 13, 2016

Pavel Datsyuk accomplished a lot during his 14 seasons in the NHL.

He helped Detroit win the Stanley Cup in 2002 and 2008. Earned three Selke trophies as the league's best defensive forward. Picked up four Lady Byng trophies for his gentlemanly and effective play.

And was part of a team that nearly managed what has become all but impossible: Winning the Cup in consecutive seasons.

His Red Wings beat the Penguins in six games in the 2008 final, then took the Penguins to seven games before losing the following season.

That's the closest any club has come to claiming back-to-back Cup titles since Detroit did it in 1997 and 1998.

The Penguins, coming off a six-game victory against the San Jose Sharks in the 2016 final, are the next team to have a chance to match that feat.

Precedent makes it clear that will be extremely difficult, and Datsyuk, who has returned to Russia to play, believes there's no mystery about why.

"There are lots of good teams," he said recently. "That's why it's tough to win."

Parity, however, isn't the only issue. The salary cap introduced in 2005 makes it almost impossible to hoard good players, and the physical demands of winning the first Cup mitigate against doing it again 12 months later.

Especially when there is another high-stakes competition, such as an Olympics or a World Cup, shoehorned between those playoff runs.

"You need so many things to go right to win," Penguins center Sidney Crosby said. "Obviously, a team has to be at the top of its game and, on top of that, you have to stay healthy and you need some bounces along the way."

Based on the past couple of decades, that is a tough trifecta to hit.

Recognizing long odds isn't the same as meekly accepting them, though.

"Just because nobody's done it doesn't mean you can't," Penguins general manager Jim Rutherford said. "That's the message we have to go by."

GM Knows the Deal

This won't the first time Rutherford has tried to win back-to-back titles. His first attempt didn't go well.

As general manager in Carolina, he built a team that captured the Cup in 2006. The Hurricanes were not able to repeat the following season. Their 40-34-8 record wasn't even good enough to get

Sidney Crosby (87) and Evgeni Malkin (71) are just two of the familiar faces at the core of a Penguins team hungry for repeat success. (Matt Freed/Post-Gazette)

them into the playoffs.

Of course, as Rutherford was quick to point out, that was a different team, in a different time.

"The hurdles there [were] different from here," he said. "We have the resources to keep much of our team intact.

"In Carolina, we lost key players. [Mark] Recchi and [Doug] Weight, and guys like that. I can't compare the two."

Familiar Cast Can Help

Significant personnel turnover in the offseason is a given for most NHL teams, particularly those that have won a Cup.

Free agents are looking to be paid for their contribution to the team's success, and there's only so much room under the salary cap.

But the Penguins, through a confluence of sound management and good luck, have returned virtually their entire team. Defenseman Ben Lovejoy, right winger Beau Bennett and goalie Jeff Zatkoff were the only players to depart via free agency over the summer.

"The fact we have a good chunk of our team back ... hopefully, that's something that can help us," Crosby said.

Rutherford made a conscious decision to not overhaul his roster — "I like the fact that we could keep as many guys as we have" — but acknowledged that teams occasionally go stale if there isn't enough turnover.

"If we need fresh blood, we'll deal with it," he said. "I like where we're at now, but we'll have to watch to see if, in fact, that carries over."

Not surprisingly, Rutherford's players see that roster stability as a plus.

"We really like our group, and we're pretty fortunate we have almost the entire group back," center Matt Cullen said.

Crosby feels the benefits of limited turnover on the roster should outweigh any negatives.

"I've seen both," he said. "I've seen a dramatic change in [the number of returning] players and that has its challenges, and then I've seen where you barely lose anyone.

"That has its advantages, as far as everyone understanding their role and making sure you're on the same page, right from the start, understanding what the coach is expecting."

Defenseman Kris Letang noted that, while the Penguins roster didn't change much over the summer, it hasn't been intact for all that long.

"We only came all together at the [trade] deadline," he said. "We had what, like a month-and-a-half and then two months of playoffs to glue together? Imagine what one year [together] can do."

The Fatigue Factor

Marian Hossa knows all about playing for the Stanley Cup.

He was with the Penguins when they lost to Detroit in the 2008 final and on the Red Wings squad the Penguins beat a year later.

After those disappointments, Hossa moved on to Chicago, where he won the Stanley Cup in 2010, 2013 and 2015.

He has appeared in 19 or more playoff games in six of the past nine seasons, so he's familiar with the grind that goes with competing for a championship. And, more to the point, its lingering effects.

"It's not easy, because you go through the extra two months [of playoff games] when you win the first Cup, then it's such a short summer," he said. "Then you go again, and teams are ready for you."

The Penguins were a popular choice to win the Cup in 2010, but Jaroslav Halak's goaltending and the collective fatigue rooted in their playoff runs the previous two years, as well as the 2010 Olympics, helped to make it possible for Montreal

Rookie Jake Guentzel would serve as an essential spark for the Penguins, both in the second half and in the playoffs. (Haley Nelson/Post-Gazette)

to upset them in the second round.

"I would say there was a little fatigue that set in," Crosby said. "That being said, it's something a lot of teams have had to deal with. It's just one of those things that you try to manage and be aware of."

Of course, there are variables that can't be predicted, such as the concussion with which Crosby was diagnosed Monday.

Ultimately, then, it wouldn't be prudent for the Penguins to enter the season focused on winning another Cup. Their goal is simply to elevate their game to the level required to win a championship, and hope they are healthy and lucky enough to get into a position to do it.

"We have to look at it the same way we would any other year," Crosby said. "Make sure we get a good start and we've got to build and get better as the year goes along." ▪

30
GOALIE

MATT MURRAY

The Natural

By Sam Werner · November 7, 2016

The first time Matt Murray put on goalie pads, he didn't exactly look like a natural. At 7 years old, wearing rented goalie equipment, Murray barely could move across the crease.

"I actually put my pads on the wrong legs," he said. "It may not seem like a big deal, but it's impossible to move it if you put them on the wrong legs because the outside is so stiff.

"I was basically just flopping around on my stomach the entire game."

He has gotten a bit more comfortable in goal since then.

Murray — who finally made his season debut last week after missing more than a month with a broken hand that occurred at the World Cup of Hockey — has developed from that kid flopping around in the crease into a Stanley Cup champion goalie.

In many ways, Murray's size and rangy athleticism make him the prototype of the modern NHL goaltender. His skill set also has put the Penguins in a well-publicized predicament, as next summer's expansion draft might force the Penguins to trade franchise cornerstone Marc-Andre Fleury if they want to keep Murray.

Those skills were developed and honed over the past 15 years, from Thunder Bay, Ontario, to Pittsburgh.

As soon as he got his pads on the right legs.

Murray spent his first hockey-playing years, ages 7-9, splitting time between defense and goalie. At age 10, he had to make a choice.

"They said I had to pick one, so I did some soul-searching, took a couple of days and decided to be a goalie," Murray said. "I think that was the right choice."

Like most kids, Murray liked all the equipment associated with playing in goal. He also liked the level of customization and personal expression the position afforded him.

"I always thought the helmets were a really cool thing," he said. "I liked to look at a lot of NHL guys' helmets back when I was younger, just because I liked the personalization of it."

Today, Murray's mask is an homage to his

Matt Murray makes a glove save on Ottawa's Zack Smith during the Eastern Conference final.
(Peter Diana/Post-Gazette)

heritage, with Dutch and Scottish flags — his parents' homelands — on the back.

Murray also liked the cerebral aspect of the sport.

"You have to have almost like a sixth sense, hockey sense," Murray said. "You could be as athletic and as fast as you want, but if you're reacting after the shot comes or after the pass is made, you're not going to get there in time."

Shortly after he started playing full time in goal, Murray caught the eye of Rick Evoy, a Peewee goaltender coach for the AAA Thunder Bay Kings, the local travel team.

When Evoy — who ended up coaching Murray through the beginning of his junior career — recalls first seeing Murray play, even at just 10 years old, his first recollection is "smooth, very smooth."

"His stance, his movement side-to-side, the way he used his stick and his gloves, it was all natural," Evoy said. "There wasn't anything forced, it was just the way he was. I noticed it at 10, and I told his parents that he is going to go far."

Around that time, Murray also began spending some time in the summer at Jon Elkin's Goalie School in Toronto. Elkin, now the goaltenders coach with the Arizona Coyotes, specifically recalled how naturally Murray could get into his butterfly technique — the standard for modern goalies, yet a potentially awkward physical position.

"There's a lot of technical details involved in executing the butterfly properly," Elkin said. "Some people have better flexibility at the hips than others, and Matt has a lot of flexibility. One can improve their flexibility, although to get to where Matt is, not everybody can get there."

And for as quickly as Murray took to the technical aspects of the position, the pure, intangible satisfaction of shutting down an opposing shooter is what made him fall in love with playing between the pipes.

"A big glove save goes a long way," Murray said. "It's kind of like golf. You know in golf, where you might hit one or two good shots a round, but those one or two good shots keep you coming back? It's kind of like a glove save being a goalie. That's probably the most fun thing about it."

Murray knows the feeling as an avid golfer himself. Growing up, he played just about every sport available to him, and was athletic enough to excel in most of them.

He enjoyed basketball as a kid, but now tennis is his preferred offseason sport. He and a group of longtime friends play in the offseason when he goes back to Thunder Bay.

Murray's coaches encouraged other sports — particularly reflex-oriented games such as tennis and racquetball — to help develop lateral quickness, hand-eye movement and response to unpredictable movement patterns.

Murray's tall, rangy frame always lent itself to these sports, too. Evoy recalled seeing Murray off to juniors — Murray was picked in the second round of the 2010 OHL draft by the Sault Ste. Marie Greyhounds — as a 6-foot-tall, 15-year-old. When he returned to Thunder Bay, he had shot up another 4 inches.

The Penguins currently list Murray at 6 feet 4, 178 pounds. Evoy joked Murray was a "beanpole" out of his equipment, especially in his later teen years. Getting Murray's weight and strength up has been a focus for Bales and the Penguins since the team selected him in the third round of 2012 NHL draft.

"Obviously, when he got in scramble situations and stuff, he wasn't as quick as he is now," Bales recalled of his scouting trips to Sault Ste. Marie to watch Murray. "He was probably a little weak and not able to move the gear around as fast as he'd like. When he was on his feet, he moved really well for a big guy. That was really impressive."

When you ask any of his current teammates about Murray's best attribute, though, the answer just about always comes back to his mental approach to the game. Murray was unflappable backstopping the Penguins to a Stanley Cup in the spring, and appeared to not miss a beat in two wins against the Ducks and the Sharks last week.

Murray always has played with confidence, his former coaches say, but it took a bit of prodding to make it a true asset for him on the ice.

Evoy, for instance, said the one area he had to work most with Murray was his willingness to come out of his net and play the puck.

"Both those efforts are totally confidence moves," Evoy said. "You have to be confident to come out of the net."

Murray's competitiveness, though, has never really been a question. Evoy recalled one game, a AAA Peewee tournament championship in Superior, Wisc., when Murray allowed a goal to tie the score with three seconds left on the clock.

After Murray got some consoling from Evoy in the locker room, the teams ended up playing six 10-minute overtimes before Murray's team ended up winning. Murray finished with 44 saves on 47 shots.

"Six overtimes," Evoy said. "Everybody was to the point of, 'Oh just let a goal in, we don't care. We're tired and we want to go home.'"

Everybody except Murray, who even admits that dealing with the frustration of getting scored on was one of his biggest challenges with learning the goalie position as he got older.

"It'd get to a point where it'd be detrimental because I was so angry about it," Murray said. "That's probably the toughest part, especially when you're young because you don't know how to control your emotions when you're young. That was the toughest part, trying to keep my cool when I kept getting scored on."

He learned to do so, though, and now draws praise for his calm demeanor on the ice, even as sticks, pucks and skates are flying around him.

Evoy credits Murray's parents, Jim Murray and Fenny Seinen, with instilling in their son a sense of maturity that carries over into his role in the Penguins' goal.

"His parents made sure he was grounded," Evoy said. "His parents had a big, big influence on his attitude in the net. You know how everybody says he's so calm? That came from his parents."

Murray's parents — with the help of another family — learned how to help him put his pads on right, too. And once they figured that out, all the pieces were in place for Murray to develop into the goalie he is today.

"It wasn't a great experience my first time," Murray said. "But for whatever reason I wanted to keep doing it." ∎

HEAD COACH

MIKE SULLIVAN

Since Joining Penguins, Sullivan Has Proven He Was Born to Coach

By Jason Mackey • December 11, 2016

It didn't take long for Mike Sullivan to impress Matt Murray.

A few minutes, tops.

"As soon as I met him, I thought, 'This guy was born to be a hockey coach,'" Murray said of Sullivan, whom he met at the Penguins development camp last July. Sullivan was hired one month earlier to coach Wilkes-Barre/Scranton to oversee the organization's top prospects, a group that at the time included Murray. "It showed with how he communicates, how he thinks the game and how he's literally always trying to find ways to give us an advantage."

In December 2015, Mike Johnston was fired, and Sullivan replaced him as head coach of the Penguins. Their Stanley Cup-winning journey was nothing short of magical, reconnecting a city with its hockey team. For Murray, it became an affirmation of what he thought all along.

If the past year has proven anything, it's that Michael Barry Sullivan, a 48-year-old Boston boy with a thick accent, a thicker belief system and sense of duty, is doing exactly what he's supposed to be doing in life.

"What I like about coaching is that it's not unlike being a schoolteacher," Sullivan said during an interview in his office at the UPMC Lemieux Sports Complex last week. "It's a teaching profession. It's managing people. It's trying to break the game down in a way that individuals and the group can comprehend."

It's a challenge Sullivan has mastered, all while relying on a direct style that has endeared him to his players. Play a bad game? Sullivan will tell you. Play a good one? He'll tell you that, too. Spend even a smidgen of time around the team, and you start to pick up the fact that what "Sully" says goes.

Johnston faltered because he couldn't connect with the Penguins' stars and coax the best out of them. Sullivan has done that and more while creating a clear identity of how the Penguins want to play, the same style that many NHL teams are now trying to emulate.

"The direction of this team was changed

Head coach Mike Sullivan shouts instructions to his team during a game against the Red Wings in the regular season. (Peter Diana/Post-Gazette)

when he got here," general manager Jim Rutherford said. "His leadership, his view of how to play the game and his communication with the players is second to none."

'I Love the Teaching Aspect'

Perhaps former Boston University coach Jack Parker saw this one coming. After all, he had a good inclination when it came to Sullivan's college career.

"I remember recruiting him and thinking, 'Not only is this kid a good player, but if comes here, he'll wind up being the captain of the team," Parker recalled.

Sullivan became that captain Parker expected, and a good one at that.

"One of the best I've ever had, no question about it," said Parker, 71, who was head coach of the Terriers for 40 years before retiring after the 2012-13 season.

Although Sullivan knew he wanted to reach the game's highest level as a player — he was drafted in the fourth round in 1987 by the New York Rangers and played 709 games for four NHL teams — coaching was always in the back of his mind. Parker was a huge reason for that.

"Jack had the biggest impression on me as a player and as a person," Sullivan said. "Part of it might have been my age; that's an impressionable age. But he was a very good teacher. He's very articulate. He ran great practices. I learned a lot when I was there.

"When I went to college, I thought I knew a lot about hockey. Then I got there, and I realized how little I knew about hockey."

As Sullivan's playing career reached its third decade, and with a couple of young kids at home, his attention started to shift to the process of preparation. How practices were structured. Specific drills. The volume of information coaches are counted upon to process.

An affinity for the most basic elements of coaching is one of the things that separates Sullivan, said Jim Johannson, assistant executive director of hockey operations for USA Hockey, which is considering Sullivan to coach its Olympic team. Some guys are enthralled by playoff victories, the Stanley Cup and money. Sullivan could be coaching players half the age of his current ones, and he'd be thrilled.

"I would be excited to be a high school hockey coach and coach 15- and 16-year-olds," Sullivan said. "I'd be excited to be a college coach.

"I love the teaching aspect. I love breaking down film and having a one-on-one conversation with a player, helping him with the details of his game."

Connecting outside the office

A few days after he replaced Johnston, Sullivan went to dinner by himself at Meat & Potatoes on Penn Avenue, Downtown. His tenure here did not have a fairytale beginning. Kris Letang was awful. Sidney Crosby was worse. The Penguins welcomed Sullivan with four consecutive losses while scoring a total of four goals.

As Sullivan sat in the restaurant, Letang walked through the front door. It turned out to be one of a few serendipitous encounters with the Penguins' most important players that helped turn the season around.

"We talked for probably 25 minutes,"

Sullivan said. "I shared some of my thoughts. He shared some of his. I think 'Tanger' and I in that conversation, we connected."

Letang was a minus-14 with one goal and 14 points in 25 games under Johnston. With Sullivan, Letang was a plus-23 with 15 goals and 53 points in 46 games during the 2015-16 regular season.

Before Sullivan arrived, Letang was a frustrated mess. Once Sullivan figured out how to let his best defenseman play to his strengths, Letang responded in such a way that he played like one of top defensemen in the league.

"You see how passionate he is, how he loves the game," Letang said. "He brought his passion and intensity to our team."

A few days later, Sullivan was at another restaurant — he doesn't remember which one — and Letang, Sidney Crosby and Pascal Dupuis showed up.

Another impromptu meeting. Another lengthy conversation about life and the state of the Penguins, wobbly as it was at the time. More trust was built.

"What's great about those moments is that everybody's guard's down because you're not coming to work," Sullivan said. "You just happened to bump into each other, and the conversation evolves.

"It didn't start on hockey, but it turned into hockey. Before you know it, a half-hour goes by, you've talked 20 of those 30 minutes about your team.

"Both sides get a chance to share their thoughts and their insights. It gave me an opportunity to get to know them a little bit and maybe what their concerns were and how they felt. I think that

helped me try to help them. I think they got a real good opportunity to get to know me and how I operate or what my personality is like. I think that's important."

Crosby's game also flourished, and this season he's the favorite for a heap of NHL hardware. Sullivan has played a big part in that.

"He's very detailed, whether that's being on time or as far as details of our game, work habits and practices, things like that," Crosby said. "He takes details really serious. I think he expects a lot out of us, and I think that's a good thing."

"Look at our 'Big Four,'" Sullivan said of Crosby, Evgeni Malkin, Phil Kessel and Letang. "They all want to skate. They all want to play fast. They don't want to slow the game down. We tried to simplify the game in a way that we could play to that strength."

Keeping key veterans, let alone coaching them, has been a change for Sullivan. In his first NHL head coaching stint, Sullivan helped the Boston Bruins win the 2003-04 Northeast Division title with 104 points.

After the 2004-05 lockout, though, the Bruins failed to sign several key players, and Sullivan was fired following a 74-point season in 2005-06.

Working as an assistant coach alongside John Tortorella with the Tampa Bay Lightning, Rangers and Vancouver Canucks afforded Sullivan the chance to coach elite talents such as Vinny Lecavalier, Martin St. Louis, Marian Gaborik and Daniel and Henrik Sedin.

What he learned along the way helped Sullivan evolve in his approach, Tortorella said.

"He's so sound with Xs and Os," Tortorella said of Sullivan this past March. "But where I think he has grown is that I think he understands how to handle the top players, which is a very important part of our business, and you have a number of them [in Pittsburgh] that are high-echelon players that he needs to mold and play under a team concept. You got the right guy there."

Away from the rink

Taking complex ideas and explaining them in an easy-to-understand way comes naturally to Sullivan. Unplugging, however, does not.

"I take it home," Sullivan admitted. "I wish I didn't as much as I do. I think it's just part of my DNA."

To manage, Sullivan relies a lot on his wife, Kate. "She's my best friend and my confidant," he said.

Walks with Kate and their two Labrador retrievers, Hank and Stanley, are one of the few ways Sullivan relaxes. That and catching up with his college-aged kids Kaitlin, Kiley and Matt over the phone.

"My family helps me unwind," Sullivan said.

But even that, Sullivan will admit, doesn't happen much. He works this much because it doesn't feel anything like work.

"On our off days I'll break down film, wondering how to help a certain player or get the power play going," Sullivan said. "In the summertime, there isn't a day that goes by that I don't think about our team or our coaching staff or how we can get better.

"It's hard for me to turn it off. I love it. I love what I do. I don't feel like it's a job. I get to go to the rink every day and do something I love."

Sullivan reads a lot and believes wholeheartedly in finding sources of inspiration outside of hockey. He's consumed several books on Bill Belichick — relax, he grew up less than an hour from Boston — and calls Tom Brady's story of beating the odds at Michigan and in the NFL "inspiring."

Stories of pro athletes who've beaten the odds or done more as a collective group than individuals are two of the things that he loves sharing with his players.

"I think some of our best teaching opportunities are outside of hockey," Sullivan said. "Our guys get so much of that every day. Sometimes I think we can spark their interest by bringing them or introducing them to something outside their world."

'He's a fair coach'

When things aren't going well, Sullivan sometimes has a hard time hiding his frustration.

During a practice in late October, he ripped into his players. David Warsofsky, who apparently took too much time tugging on a new sweater, got an earful from Sullivan.

"I didn't know it took that long to change jerseys," Sullivan shouted.

This past Wednesday, Sullivan rode Malkin during a power play drill, questioning his effort along the half-wall.

When players struggle, no matter which ones, and no matter the setting, they're told about it in no uncertain terms.

"He tells you exactly how he sees it," defenseman Ian Cole said. "It's not personal, but it's honest."

And it's appreciated.

"He's a fair coach," Carl Hagelin said. "He's going to say what he thinks. If you're playing bad, he's going to let you know. If you're playing well, he's going to let you know. That's the type of coach you want."

Mike Sullivan's detailed, direct approach to coaching has proven popular with this Penguins team. (Peter Diana/Post-Gazette)

Told that the majority of his players feel this way, that his brutal honesty is appreciated, Sullivan cracks a rare smile, like a dad whose son just brought home straight A's. Sullivan isn't the coddling type, but he always wants his players to know that he cares.

"I think my relationships with these guys are critically important to our ability to have success," Sullivan said. "I push them hard. I think the only way I'm able to push them hard, and they respond the right way, is because they know I care."

Parker said he kept a sign in his office at BU that might explain how Sullivan deals with his players. It reads: "Kids don't care how much you know until they know how much you care."

Sullivan tries to live by those words.

"We're a transparent coaching staff," Sullivan said. "We don't believe in sweeping anything under the rug. We're not always warm and fuzzy. That's just part of my personality.

"My hope is that the players get to know us, know me and understand that our motivation is simply to help them be at their best and help this team win." ∎

71
FORWARD

EVGENI MALKIN

Quietly Thriving

By Jason Mackey · January 8, 2017

Sidney Crosby's projected goal total sits in the low 60s, and he's regularly flirting with 20-year-old records. Justin Schultz had six goals and 18 points in December alone, the best month for a Penguins defenseman this side of Sergei Zubov, while barging his way into the All-Star Game conversation.

Too bad for Evgeni Malkin. All he did was lead the NHL in total points (21) and assists (14), walking away empty-handed in only four of 15 games while ascending to the top of the NHL scoring race before last week's break.

"I feel like I have a lot of energy," Malkin said. "I work hard every game and want to be the top forward every game."

Malkin has been the Penguins' top forward for a large chunk this season, even if Crosby's goal-scoring binge has generated more headlines, some of that stemming from his stature league-wide. But Malkin, his own penalty-taking spree at the start of the season aside, has found a way to rewind his game to levels last seen in 2011-12 and previous to that.

In short, it's the best Geno we've seen in some time.

The biggest thing that stands out, Malkin's teammates will tell you, has been his consistency. He's bringing it every shift. Even — absurd as it may seem — on the defensive end. The longest he's gone without scoring has been a grand total of two games.

"He plays the right way on both sides of the puck," linemate Patric Hornqvist said. "This year he's been really good for us. I think that started last year when [coach Mike Sullivan] took over. Sully always says you have to play the right way to get chances. Usually the best defense turns into the best offense. The way he's playing right now, it's fun to watch. It's fun to be a part of."

Malkin has 16 goals and 43 points in 38 games entering today's 5 p.m. start against the Lightning. Over 82 games, that's a 35-goal and 93-point pace. It would represent Malkin's most productive season since he had 50 goals and 109 points in 2011-12.

There have been 11 games this season where

Evgeni Malkin breaks away from the check of Senators left winger Alexandre Burrows during the Eastern Conference final. (Peter Diana/Post-Gazette)

Malkin hasn't scored, 28.9 percent. That's the best for him since finding the scoresheet in 45 of 60 games in 2013-14. In 2011-12, Malkin scored in 60 of 75, which means he went without a point a career-low 20 percent of the time.

"He's so hard to handle with his size, with his hands, the way he sees the ice," Crosby said. "He's been so consistent. That's been a big part of our success in the month of December. Him making the difference on different plays or different games, whether it be setting up plays or putting the puck in himself."

Why's it Working?

A few factors paint the picture of Malkin's consistency in 2016-17.

First, health. Malkin injured his left elbow March 11 of last season in a 3-2 win at Columbus. He was never fully healthy and had to play with a brace. Despite not having offseason surgery, the elbow has not bothered Malkin this season, and he's not wearing a brace.

"I forget [that ever happened]," Malkin said. "Nothing sore, nothing bad. It's good. No brace anymore. Last year was so hard to play with a big, huge brace. Now it's just amazing, no brace, nothing's sore, I'm just excited to play."

Second was Malkin's offseason. He's 30 now and still draws plenty of laughs when referring to himself as old. Self-deprecation aside, Malkin tweaked his offseason routine to focus more on leg work. He has also started working more with Andy O'Brien, who's the Penguins director of sport science and performance.

"I had a good summer," Malkin said. "Always if you work hard in the summer, it helps you in the season. I worked with Andy a little bit. He gave me a program. I started to work on my legs a little bit more. When you're old, you need to work a little bit more on your legs. I feel pretty good."

As he has previously admitted, Malkin was angry — though he didn't use that word — at himself following a lackluster performance in the World Cup of Hockey. He felt he didn't play with the puck enough. Without falling down the analytics rabbit hole, the puck-possession differences have been night and day.

Malkin has also cut it out when it comes to penalties. After accumulating 36 penalty minutes in his first 20 games, he has just 10 in his last 18. It's a little tough to score when you're in the penalty box.

Bigger Picture Adjustments

Former Penguin Ruslan Fedotenko was in town Saturday for the reunion of the 2009 Stanley Cup-winning team and planned to dine with Malkin later in the day.

Fedotenko, now retired and living in Tampa, has noticed several changes in Malkin, one of them his command of English and his willingness to use it.

"He was pretty quiet in English," Fedotenko said during Saturday's practice. "He was pretty loud in Russian, and outspoken. I was like, 'Geno, nobody understands you except me and [Sergei Gonchar].'"

Also, maturity. Malkin talked Friday about how being 7-month-old Nikita's dad has changed him. No more restaurants. No more quiet time at home. A lot of chasing the ever-mobile Nikita. Fedotenko can see fatherhood having an effect, too.

Evgeni Malkin clashes with Senators players in Game 5 of the Eastern Conference final. After a slew of late-season injuries, Malkin powered back with a vengeance during the playoffs. (Matt Freed/Post-Gazette)

"He had that personality, goofy, like a kid, and now he's a dad," Fedotenko said. "He definitely matured. He's still kind of kept that persona between us and how he jokes and everything else, but obviously he knows when it's mature time, and when he needs to be more grown-up."

On the ice, Malkin has seemingly adjusted how he goes about his business. At least in terms of not forcing things and playing a smarter game.

"He's not trying to do too much himself," Fedotenko said. "Sometimes I remember the team would be struggling and he's just trying to do too much himself. He learned how he can make other players even better. He's so good, he makes all the players around him even better. As long as he sticks with that, he's so effective. He learned how to use that on a consistent basis."

Apparently scoring isn't the only thing Malkin has been doing with regularity. ■

87
FORWARD

SIDNEY CROSBY

en It Comes to Giving, the Penguins Captain Does as Much as He Can

By Jason Mackey • February 12, 2017

It's hardly uncommon for Penguins president/CEO David Morehouse to escort a group of kids into the home team's dressing room at PPG Paints Arena after a game. Not to talk or celebrate, simply to soak in the scene.

During one particular game last year, Morehouse had to step out and instructed the group to stay off to the side and not bother anyone. But when he returned, the kids weren't keeping quiet in the corner.

They were getting quizzed by Penguins captain Sidney Crosby.

"He was asking if they played hockey, who they played for, if they won their last game," Morehouse said. "And it's not stuff that's coming out because he has to. He's genuinely interested."

Sidney Crosby will soon reach 1,000 NHL points, but that doesn't come close to fully painting the picture of a polite, humble and strikingly thoughtful native of Cole Harbour, Nova Scotia.

"People from my hometown have always made it a point to give back," Crosby said. "I always told myself that, if I ever get to this point, I would do the same.

"I think a lot of guys have the same approach. You feel lucky to do what you do. If you can help out in other ways, and this puts you in that position, you try to do your best."

Crosby and Penguins co-owner Mario Lemieux once shared a roof, so it should come as no surprise that they share a philosophy when it comes to doing good deeds.

Both are happy to help and legitimately enjoy it, but Crosby, like Lemieux, makes it a point to carve out some one-on-one time, to ensure that whomever he's hosting or helping knows he's not doing it for the attention.

"It's not about that at all for him," said Penguins director of communications Jen Bullano.

She would certainly know.

In 2011, Crosby was out of the lineup with a concussion, and the Penguins made their annual visit to Children's Hospital.

Crosby got along so well with one boy there and was so touched that he later asked Bullano to go back ... just the two of them, no cameras, no attention.

When Bullano and Crosby met for the follow-up visit, Crosby appeared clutching a pair of Toys

Penguins captain Sidney Crosby celebrates in the wake of Chris Kunitz's game-winning goal in the second overtime of Game 7 against the Senators. (Matt Freed/Post-Gazette)

"R" Us bags, filled with a Transformer toy the two had discussed.

"He literally bought every type of this toy they make," Bullano said. "[Crosby] had never seen it before and thought it was so cool.

"There are no pictures of this. There's no video. He was laying in the bed with the kid. They were just playing. We were there for over two hours. I got to know the mom really well because we were just sitting there.

"The kid had no idea. Didn't expect it. They had no idea he was coming. We got there and he said, 'Hey buddy. hope you don't mind that I came back.' The kid couldn't believe it.

"[Crosby's] crazy cool about stuff like that."

What's crazy is trying to recount the many times stuff like this has happened with Crosby:

• The Little Penguins Learn to Play program has been around for nine seasons, outfitting now 1,200 kids with free head-to-toe hockey equipment. Not only does Crosby serve as the face of the program — which the NHL has now adopted — but he helps fund it, too.

"There's an awareness of what a person in his position can bring," Penguins vice president of communications Tom McMillan said. "I think he activates that as much as anybody I've seen during his playing career."

• After a recent practice, Crosby noticed a local family in the Penguins dressing room, approached them, introduced himself, learned their story and wound up giving them a signed stick.

Nobody asked Crosby to do that, and he wanted zero credit when discussing it a couple days later.

"For people who have the opportunity to come in here, people dealing with certain things, if you can brighten their day a bit or spend some time with them, it's something that's special for all of us," Crosby said.

• A few years ago, through a team charity event, Crosby befriended a 4-year-old Amish boy with cancer. Crosby remarked to Bullano how much he loved talking to the boy because of how engaging the boy was and how he wasn't consumed with technology. Crosby even tried to visit the boy but learned he had passed away.

• He learns the first and last names of the kids who attend his hockey school in Cole Harbour, Nova Scotia.

"Two kids came from Japan its first year," Bullano recalled. "He was so blown away by that. He couldn't wait to meet them."

• Earlier this season, the Penguins welcomed Grant Chupinka, 24-year-old cancer patient, into the dressing room. Crosby chatted up Grant and his parents, Steve and Kim.

He spent his usual time — about two or three times the requirement. Gave the tour. Then found out the Chupinkas didn't have tickets for that night's game and decided he would pay for them to go.

"I'm sure he could just give them an autographed puck or something, but he takes his time to go out and see them and talk to them and get to know them," Brian Dumoulin said. "It speaks volumes for him and who he is as a person."

Spend any length of time with Crosby during his visits with those less fortunate, and a few things become obvious.

Sidney Crosby shares a laugh with goalie Marc-Andre Fleury (not pictured) during practice. (Peter Diana/Post-Gazette)

One, Crosby is really good at these. Smooth but not in a slimy way. Sweet. You know how when you're around someone talking and they go out of their way to make eye contact with everyone around? That's Crosby.

He's also humble, always introducing himself like those he's meeting don't already know. Holding a hand is no issue. And Crosby is the rare 20-something pro athlete without kids who acts every bit like he does.

"It is not an easy situation to talk to someone with terminal cancer," McMillan said. "A lot of people couldn't do that. He has an amazing ability to do that and make that person feel good."

Crosby has welcomed several Make-a-Wish kids and tries, if at all possible, to schedule such events for practice days — to maximize the time he's able to spend.

He's developed a special friendship with Patrick McIlvain, a soldier who nearly died when he took a bullet to the head in Afghanistan. McIlvain actually does physical therapy with one of Crosby's sticks.

A former club hockey player at Cal U, McIlvain comes by every year, and the Penguins don't even bother to tell Crosby. Either he already knows or immediately stops what he's doing to come say hello.

"He's not doing it to leave a legacy," said Terry Kalna, Penguins vice president of sales and broadcasting. "His numbers leave the legacy. He's just a down-to-Earth, good guy."

Before a visit, Crosby has Bullano email him what is essentially a scouting report on who he's going to meet. He likes to learn about them, their situation and what they've been through. As much information as he can ingest. Crosby never just swoops in, shake a hand and leave.

"As much as anyone has ever seen, he accepts the responsibilities of being not just a professional athlete but a star professional athlete," McMillan said. "He views it as part of the job. Like coming to the morning skate. That's just what you do."

Put another way, "he owns those moments," says Kalna.

Said Bullano, "He's just a good human being."

There are also the stories of humility from within the team. When Carter Rowney was called up for the first time, he was taken aback when Crosby dropped in on his workout to chat.

"Someone like him and he included me?" Rowney wondered aloud. "I didn't know him or anything like that. It was cool to see him come over and say hi."

Scott Wilson remembers waiting in line for preseason photos a couple of years ago when Crosby, with a jam-packed schedule, was told to jump in line.

"Sid actually turned to me and said, 'Is it OK if I got ahead?' " Wilson said. "Little things like that."

The most astounding, though, is the charity work. Some that the Penguins ask him to do, as much or more that they don't. It would make Roberto Clemente proud as a charitable ambassador of Pittsburgh.

"We couldn't ask for anyone better or anything more, both on and off the ice," Morehouse said. "As a hockey player and as a leader, we literally hit the lottery with Sidney Crosby.

"He's the person we've built the team around. He's the person we built the brand around. Built a new arena because of. The off-the-ice stuff was instrumental in the growth of youth hockey in Western Pennsylvania. It's a good illustration of our ownership's commitment to giving back to the community.

"He exemplifies who we are to the very core." ∎

Sidney Crosby is introduced as the No. 1 star after notching his 1,000th career point on Feb. 18 at PPG Paints Arena. (Matt Freed/Post-Gazette)

One Grand Night

With His Parents in the Building, Sidney Crosby Reaches 1,000 Points

By Jason Mackey • February 16, 2017

Few things on this planet mean as much to Sidney Crosby as his mother, Trina, but there's no way he planned this.

While Sidney was stuck one or two points shy of 1,000 for his career since Feb. 7, Trina was stuck in Nova Scotia, unable to get out because of a snowstorm.

Her son's historic performance Thursday — a goal and two assists in a 4-3 overtime win against the Jets at PPG Paints Arena, surpassing the 1,000-point plateau in the process — was definitely worth the wait.

Although Sidney Crosby could have gone without the added discussion his lack of puck luck generated.

"You want to get it," he said. "It's a great number, but it's not something you want to talk about for a week, week and a half. That means that you're probably not putting it in that much.

"We had lots of chances the last few games. I could tell guys were looking for me a little bit more. I appreciate it, but I'm glad they don't have to think about it or answer about it."

No more answers about that, but Crosby was asked to talk about an emotional moment that played out in the first period Thursday after he set up Chris Kunitz on a workmanlike play at 6:28.

Crosby out-skated Blake Wheeler to a loose puck, fed Kunitz in the slot and eventually was able to exhale.

A standing ovation ensued. Marc-Andre Fleury left his crease to offer a congratulatory pat on the back. In the stands, tears filled his father Troy's eyes. On the ice, the proud native of Cole Harbour, Nova Scotia, acknowledged the reception by raising his stick.

"It's pretty emotional," Crosby said. "You start to look up at the Jumbotron. You see all of those things. They go by pretty quick. You're flashing all of these different plays and years. That's how fast it feels, when you're looking at it."

What didn't feel fast for Crosby was the wait.

He had chances. His line with Kunitz and Jake Guentzel was plenty productive. They simply weren't going in. And Crosby was getting asked more and more about shooting for 1,000.

"He could have been done way earlier than that," Kris Letang said. "We didn't care about it. Sid is a guy that doesn't focus on that. The team winning is more important than anything for him."

"I was happy to be there [on the ice] with him," Fleury added. "I'm so proud of him. I have a lot of respect for this guy. He's a good friend. He's a great captain. He works hard, and he deserves it."

The team won when Crosby nudged a puck past Jets goaltender Connor Hellebuyck at 4:38 of overtime, and it kept the Penguins (36-13-7) perfect when leading after two periods since the start of last season.

They're now 63-0 in those situations.

That Crosby's 1,000th point came this way speaks volumes about Crosby's style as a player. Sure, he possesses immense, obvious skill. The best the NHL has seen since he was drafted. But Crosby's skill doesn't go anywhere without his tireless work ethic riding shotgun.

"He knows where everybody is on the ice,"

Sidney Crosby serves the puck to Chris Kunitz for the assist and his 1,000th career point. (Matt Freed/Post-Gazette)

Kunitz said. "When you can slide off and make space, he's going to look for that person who's coming toward him and slide it to that guy by him. He puts it right in your wheelhouse."

Another part of Crosby's game that is continually on-point is his laser focus. Few things distract him. It's what makes him so elite; whether it's off the ice and in his personal life or in the middle of games. He finds a zone and doesn't leave.

Which is why what occurred following the milestone moment was even more special.

Crosby took a minute to look around, to recognize what the moment meant. He doesn't do that often.

"You really try to soak in moments like that," Crosby said.

He said it's "right up there" when ranking the most special things he's experienced in Pittsburgh. The Penguins roaring back from a 3-2 deficit in the third starting with a power-play goal from Phil Kessel, then Crosby finishing it, only made it that much sweeter.

"It's nice to win the game," Crosby said. "When you have a memorable night like this, you want it to finish the right way."

After a rocky second period that sent the Penguins down to four defensemen because of injuries to Justin Schultz and Olli Maatta, the Penguins did finish the right way.

And Trina Crosby got to see it all in person.

"There was a storm back home, so she couldn't get here for the prior games," Sidney Crosby said. "I'm glad that I could get it done with her here." ■

29
GOALIE

MARC-ANDRE FLEURY

One Last Shot?

By Sam Werner • May 17, 2017

Andre Fleury has one rule during games: No talking.

There's some chit-chat here and there, but for the most part Monday night, the focus was exclusively on the TV, as Andre's son, Marc-Andre, and his Penguin teammates tried to win Game 2 of the Eastern Conference final and even their series against Ottawa.

So even when Maya, the dog, saw a cat behind the house and started barking, she got an, "Ah, shh!" from Andre, watching from the couch in a gray Penguins sweatshirt.

There's one topic, in particular, that Andre Fleury had no desire to hear about Monday. When a television commentator brought up the idea that Marc-Andre could be heading to the expansion Vegas Golden Knights this off-season, Andre scoffed and waved his hand at the television.

He knows Penguins general manager Jim Rutherford has a big decision on his hands this off-season — the Penguins likely will part ways with Fleury in favor of the younger, less costly Matt Murray — but now is not the time. The Penguins

are in the midst of a playoff run, halfway toward the franchise's fifth Stanley Cup. And Marc-Andre, a year after watching most of the postseason from the bench, is playing the best hockey of his career.

There will come a time to address Marc-Andre's future with the only NHL organization he has ever known. But for now — just like fans in Marc-Andre's adopted hometown of Pittsburgh — those who know him best are just trying to enjoy these moments.

* * * *

In Sorel-Tracy, about an hour northeast of Montreal, there's not much fanfare for arguably the city's most famous native son.

No "Welcome to Sorel-Tracy, Home of Marc-Andre Fleury" sign. No plaque or marker in Parc Regard-sur-le-Fleuve, where Fleury hoisted the Stanley Cup in 2009, or in Royal Square, where he brought the Cup again last summer. But there are some markers from Fleury's upbringing and hockey career.

There's the end of Rue Olympique — around

Marc-Andre Fleury makes a save against the Capitals during the Eastern Conference semifinals in Pittsburgh. (Peter Diana/Post-Gazette)

the corner from the house where Fleury grew up — which dead-ends into a cornfield. This small street, occupied almost exclusively by Fleury's aunts and uncles, is where Marc-Andre and his younger sister, Marylene, started playing street hockey.

The last house on the street, still owned by Fleury's uncle, has a garage door that took a beating when Marc-Andre started to practice his shooting, before he switched to goalie.

Of course, maybe there doesn't need to be any sort of grand public marker for Marc-Andre. This is Sorel-Tracy, a steel town of about 35,000 on the banks of the St. Lawrence River. There's no need to remind everyone that Marc-Andre Fleury is from here.

"We are a small city," Marylene said. "So everybody knows Marc."

While Sorel-Tracy doesn't have many tributes to Marc-Andre Fleury, a small bedroom on the second floor of Andre Fleury's house stands out.

There, lining the walls are photos, jerseys and other memorabilia from Marc-Andre's playing career. It's not just Marc-Andre, though. It's Marc-Andre as a Pittsburgh Penguin.

The walls are painted with black and gold stripes, and the Penguins' logo dominates the room.

Andre doesn't want to think much about what he would do with photos and jerseys from a new team if his son plays elsewhere next season.

"Maybe another room," he said.

"It would be strange to see him in another uniform, for sure," Marylene added. "He's been a Penguin for so long."

It's more than just a new uniform and team, of course. Marc-Andre, the longest-tenured player on the Penguins, has ingrained himself in the Pittsburgh community in the 14 years since the Penguins drafted him No. 1 overall in 2003.

On the wall near the door to Andre's house hangs a series of photos from the UPMC commercial featuring Marc-Andre, his wife, Veronique, and their two daughters, Estelle and Scarlett.

Sorel-Tracy is his birthplace but, even Marylene admits, Pittsburgh is his home.

* * * *

A few minutes before the Penguins' first playoff game against Columbus, Marylene was flicking through the channels and tuned in to a surprise.

She watches most Penguins games through the NHL Center Ice package, making sure to never miss one of her brother's starts — which, admittedly, weren't as frequent as he would've liked this season.

It looked like it would once again be Matt Murray in net for the postseason, but then:

"I came back to hockey and I saw my brother in net," Marylene recalled. "I was like, 'What's going on?'"

Her brother was a late replacement for Murray, unavailable with a lower-body injury.

"He was not supposed to start," Marylene said of her brother. "But you never know what's going to happen, and I think he responded very well."

While the family has enjoyed watching Marc-Andre play more, that also brings a bit more pressure to each game.

"The seventh game against Washington," Andre said. "It was stressful."

Marylene was there in person, having made the 10-hour drive from Sorel-Tracy to

Washington for the game.

"A lot of red jerseys around me," she said. "It was just fun to see him after the game. He was laughing. I know we were happy."

Had the Penguins lost, that game could've been Marc-Andre's last as a Penguin. But when Marylene saw her brother afterward, the future was the last thing on his mind.

"I think he is embracing the moment and enjoying it," she said.

Marc-Andre wasn't the only one enjoying the moment Monday night, as the Penguins closed out a 1-0 victory to tie the series.

After watching his son make a flurry of saves in the final 30 seconds to secure the win, Andre let out a laugh. Hey, in a postseason run that has seemingly been defined by Marc-Andre's smile behind his mask, like father like son, right?

"When players score goals, they like to laugh," Andre said. "So when Marc stops the puck, he's laughing, too."

And Marc-Andre has certainly been doing plenty of laughing during this playoff run — from his Game 7 stop of an Alex Ovechkin one-timer to another playoff shutout win Monday night, the 10th of his career.

"I was so happy for him," Marylene said.

The Penguins are now seven wins away from Sorel-Tracy playing host to the Stanley Cup this summer for a third time. It may be a bit early to start planning that celebration but, if it comes, it would be the most meaningful one yet.

* * *

If the Cup comes back to Sorel-Tracy, it likely would be after Fleury's future is decided. That could be a bittersweet but fitting end to his time in Pittsburgh.

He was drafted in 2003 to a team teetering on the brink of survival, and helped them win a Stanley Cup just six years later. He endured playoff struggles and took on a reputation as a playoff bust. He lost his starting job in 2016, just as the team embarked on another Stanley Cup run.

In Fleury's likely final Pittsburgh chapter, he returned as a playoff hero this postseason.

Realistically, Fleury will likely be playing in another NHL city next season, wearing a different uniform. But realism is a problem for the off-season.

"I just want him to be happy," Marylene said. "I know he needs to play. That's what he likes the most, so I want him to have many more successful years and to have fun." ■

Let the Madness Begin

Penguins Hope Their 'Weird Year' Ends in a Familiar Fashion
By Dave Molinari · April 12, 2017

The Penguins just completed their 50th regular season in the NHL.

In some ways, it was much like the 49 that preceded it.

There were games, home and road. Lots of artificial ice. Victories. Defeats.

And, uh, that should just about cover it.

For while no season ever is identical to another, 2016-17 seemed particularly unusual for the Penguins.

Perhaps that can be blamed on injuries. After all, the Penguins lost 286 man-games, virtually all to players who fill significant roles. The total includes 41 missed by Kris Letang, the cornerstone of their defense corps; Washington's entire team sat out just seven more than he did.

It could be that their abbreviated offseason, a byproduct of a Stanley Cup run last spring, played a part, too.

And the compressed schedule necessitated by last fall's World Cup of Hockey tournament likely figured in there somewhere, too.

"In a lot of ways, given all those circumstances, it's been a unique season," coach Mike Sullivan said, ignoring the possibility that voodoo dolls and/or planetary alignment might have had a major role.

Either would be as good an explanation as any for a season in which, among other oddities, the:

- Best set-up man in the game, Sidney Crosby, didn't even lead his team in assists, but instead scored more goals than anyone in the NHL.

- Line that became all but legendary in the 2016 playoffs — remember HBK? — didn't come close to making it through this season intact.

- Guy who did lead the team in assists, Phil Kessel, is a reliable goal-scorer who found the net precisely two times in the final 26 games of the regular season.

Few were predicting any of that six or seven months ago.

Sullivan and his staff, though, understood hurdles would appear over the course of the season, even if they couldn't anticipate precisely what all of them would be. Consequently, they had brainstorming sessions to consider the possibilities.

"In the big picture, some of the conversation revolved around trying to predict potential upcoming challenges, coming off a Stanley Cup championship and how we'd handle those," Sullivan said. "There were some that we could predict, and then there were others that were unforeseen."

Probably more of the latter, although the Penguins did a pretty fair job of dealing with adversities they couldn't have foreseen.

"It's been a weird year," winger Conor Sheary

said. "But we're in a good spot."

True enough. Despite the obstacles — and weirdness — the Penguins faced during the regular season, they finished with the second-most points [111] in the league and in franchise history.

It wasn't enough to earn a division title — Washington, the only team to finish with more points, also works out of the Metropolitan — but did give the Penguins home-ice advantage in their opening-round playoff series against Columbus.

That's an edge they had during Round 1 in two of their previous three title defenses.

The exception was 1992, when they were coming off a regular season that made the one just completed seem tranquil and orderly.

The 1991-92 season began with tragedy — shortly before the start of training camp, coach Bob Johnson was diagnosed with the brain tumors that would claim his life a few months later — and was pockmarked by turmoil.

"When you start rattling off what we went through in '91-92, those were bizarre circumstances," said radio analyst Phil Bourque, a left winger on that club.

The Penguins stumbled to a 5-6-3 start under Scott Bowman, who succeeded Johnson as coach, and dramatically altered their roster in a three-team trade Feb. 19. General manager Craig Patrick sent away two key members of the 1991 Cup champions, Mark Recchi and Paul Coffey, and brought in Rick Tocchet, Kjell Samuelsson, Ken Wregget and Jeff Chychrun.

That deal came during a 2-10-3 slide that precipitated the event that transformed their season.

Bowman, whose approach to interpersonal relationships with his personnel was not to be confused with Johnson's, was away visiting his family in Buffalo, when Patrick and the players gathered in a Calgary hotel ballroom in early March to discuss why a talented team that won a championship the previous spring was in mortal peril of missing the playoffs.

The focus eventually fell on Bowman, and Patrick, after absorbing his players' grievances, agreed to go to Bowman to try to find a common ground that would satisfy everyone.

The Penguins subsequently beat the Flames, 6-3, triggering an 11-5-1 run to end the season. A few months later — after surviving a 3-1 deficit against Washington in Round 1 — they claimed their second Cup.

"The crossroads of our season were in that meeting room in the hotel in Calgary," Bourque said. "It was such a cleansing moment for the players."

Although the 2016-17 Penguins haven't had to deal with that kind of personal drama, Bourque believes they could benefit from the challenges they've faced.

"This could all be good for this team," he said. "All the hurdles we had to get over in '92, I think, made us stronger, made us more battle-tested.

"I think it paid dividends in the playoffs, because we'd been through so much. Playing the Washington Capitals in the playoffs paled in comparison to all the [stuff] we had gone through during the year."

So, peculiar as it has been at times, 2016-17 won't go down as the Penguins' most unusual season that followed a Cup championship.

"I don't know if it's weird, or if it's just different," defenseman Brian Dumoulin said. "Obviously, we weren't going to have the same year we did last year."

They can only hope that it has the same ending. ◾

4

DEFENSEMAN

JUSTIN SCHULTZ

Defenseman Steps Up to Assume Role Typically
Filled by Injured Kris Letang

By Sean Gentille • May 26, 2017

I t'd be unfair to say all that much about the Penguins' continued playoff survival is a surprise. At its core, we're all still talking about a team built around Sidney Crosby and Evgeni Malkin, and a team that won a Stanley Cup a little less than 12 months ago. As of Thursday, after their Game 7 overtime win against Ottawa, they're four wins away from another.

Nobody should be shocked by any of this. Not anymore. Coach Mike Sullivan's success percentage on button-pushing is somewhere in the low 90s. We're in Year 2 of Bryan Rust's springtime morph into a top-line winger. Jake Guentzel's coming-out party was the Blue Jackets series, which feels like it happened sometime during the Bush administration.

The goalie stuff is ... the goalie stuff. Again, people are feeling bad for Marc-Andre Fleury, and again, Matt Murray is proving that sentimentality doesn't count for much. So, yes, we've seen most of this movie already — except last time, it starred Kris Letang.

It's impossible to truly replace Letang. It's amazing that the Penguins have come sufficiently close. And, if you have any sense of the circumstances that landed him here last season, it's still, frankly, weird that Justin Schultz is leading the way.

Schultz, back in the lineup for the first time since injuring his upper body in Game 2, was the Penguins' best defenseman on Friday night. He scored, too — on the Penguins' only power play of the game, at 11:44 of the third period — and generally did what he's done intermittently this season; function as a slightly off-brand version of Letang.

There's no other defenseman with a right-handed shot. Nobody else is as comfortable starting the attack at 5-on-5. Nobody else can skate like Schultz. And if he's inferior to Letang elsewhere, that's fine — most players are. But if it's a committee job to replace the sort of alpha-dog defenseman that every cap-era champ has had in common, Schultz deserves a whole lot of the credit.

Justin Schultz celebrates assisting on a goal by fellow defenseman Trevor Daley (6). Schultz tallied 39 assists in the regular season to go with his 12 goals. (Peter Diana/Post-Gazette)

In the regular season, Schultz led the Penguins defense in goals, with 12; nobody else had more than five. He led them in points, with 51; nobody else had more than 34, and that was Letang, who played 41 games before a neck injury ended his season Feb. 21.

Even before Letang exited for good, though, Schultz had begun to deliver on the promise he showed at the University of Wisconsin and in his first season with the Oilers. He's always had the skill. Now, he's got the trust of his coach.

If Schultz's first partial season with the Penguins was about rebuilding his confidence and sheltering him from difficult matchups, his second was about taking off the training wheels. The risk potential is still present, but his decision-making has improved more than enough. Now, his skills can take center stage. Nobody is waiting for the mistakes.

"I think [the goal against Ottawa], in and of itself, is an indication of the impact he has on our team and our ability to win games. But it doesn't just stop there on the power play," Sullivan said.

"He's a good puck mover. He's a mobile guy. He gets back to pucks. He sees the ice well. He can go tape-to-tape when the opportunities are there. So he helps our transition game."

In Game 7, no Penguins defenseman had a larger positive effect on puck possession; with Schultz on the ice at even-strength, the Penguins controlled more than 65 percent of all shot attempts (23-12) and out-chanced the Senators 10-5.

Again, this is from a guy who was too banged up to play two days earlier.

"He's a special hockey player. If he's not playing at 100 percent and plays a game like that, I can't wait to see him at 100 percent and hopefully in a couple days, because he was special tonight," partner Ian Cole said.

"What he does with the puck is, in my mind, second to none. Just a great offensive talent and so solid defensively as well. I can't say enough great things about him."

It's more than just fighting through a shoulder issue, or broken ribs, or whatever is bothering Schultz at the moment, though. Really — look at how hard he washed out in Edmonton. He came up through a toxic, broken system that he chose to join, so there was more than enough blame to spread around. Still, one analyst on TSN's 2016 trade deadline TV broadcast, after the Penguins acquired Schultz for a third-round pick, suggested that he was the worst player in the league.

That wasn't true — but it would've been equally silly to suggest that he'd be the leading defensive scorer on a conference champion within a year.

Here we are, though. The Penguins are four wins from doing what seemed unthinkable without Letang. They need Justin Schultz to help get them there — and if nothing else, he's shown that he's capable of getting it done. ■

Goalie Matt Murray is congratulated by Justin Schultz after the Penguins beat the Hurricanes on April 2. (Peter Diana/Post-Gazette)

Eastern Conference Quarterfinals, Game 1

APRIL 12, 2017 · PITTSBURGH, PENNSYLVANIA
PENGUINS 3, BLUE JACKETS 1

Fleury Back in Star Role

After Murray Is Last-Minute Scratch, Veteran Backstops Win

By Jason Mackey

It was almost as if the Penguins took the playoff blueprint they used last season and tucked it away somewhere deep inside PPG Paints Arena, where only coach Mike Sullivan and a few select others could see it.

Without the guy you would prefer to start in goal for Game 1? No big deal. Marc-Andre Fleury, come on down.

Bad first period? Don't sweat it. There's always the second.

Bryan Rust, Phil Kessel and Nick Bonino ... of course they're going to score postseason goals.

The Penguins followed a familiar script en route to a 3-1 victory over the Columbus Blue Jackets in Game 1 of their first-round playoff series Wednesday night at PPG Paints Arena, the same one they used to capture the franchise's fourth Stanley Cup last spring.

"Great feeling," Fleury, the Game 1 hero after stopping 31 of 32 starts in a surprise start for the injured Matt Murray, gushed at the podium afterward. "A fun game to win."

In this sequel, Fleury played the part of Jeff Zatkoff, the likable good soldier, the guy who smiled his way through a difficult situation, the goaltender who unexpectedly was thrust into duty in a key spot.

Fleury found out he was starting when he left the ice after warmup. Goaltending coach

Mike Bales broke the news that Murray tweaked a lower-body injury with about eight minutes to go, one likely lingering from the Penguins' April 6 game in New Jersey.

"I just tried to approach it as a result game," Fleury said. "Tried to be ready for it."

No problem there, the same as Rust, Kessel and Bonino being ready for the postseason. Perhaps it's etched into their contracts, the extra responsibility they assume and the other level they find this time of year.

Kessel snapped a shot past a helpless Sergei Bobrovsky — a likely Vezina Trophy finalist, mind you — and kicked another to Rust, proving to be an unlikely hero in two sports.

"The puck was kind of at my feet," Kessel explained. "I saw Rusty coming in and tried to get it in the area. ... It was kind of lucky."

Most encouraging for the Penguins as this series progresses could be the 10 shots Kessel attempted and the seven he put on goal, both team-highs.

Sullivan has urged Kessel to shoot more. It finally appears he is listening. If Kessel can conjure the 10 goals, 22 points he produced last postseason, look out.

"We know we have a team that can score on any line," Bonino said. "When we do that, we're hard to beat."

Penguins captain Sidney Crosby skates up ice during Game 1 against the Blue Jackets. The 2016-17 season marked the 10th postseason appearance in Crosby's career. (Peter Diana/Post-Gazette)

Bonino stretched the Penguins lead to 3-0 at 16:25 of the second with a dirty goal in front of Bobrovsky, who entered this one 3-5-1 in his past nine games in Pittsburgh with a 3.31 goals-against average and a .902 save percentage.

That the Penguins, who struggled early, took things over the middle period should not come as a surprise. They scored an NHL-high 106 goals in the 20 last season and led the league again with 102 in 2016-17.

Matt Calvert took advantage of a failed clear and converted from the slot at 12:41 of the third, but the Penguins turned in a mostly sound defensive effort, going two for two on the penalty kill, blocking 22 shots and keeping Fleury's crease clear.

Possessing the puck with any sort of regularity was an issue for the Penguins early. The Blue Jackets outshot the Penguins, 16-3, in the first period, although Sullivan sensed a momentum change with about three minutes to go.

"The last three minutes, we got some real commitment to playing defense," Sullivan said. "Guys were blocking shots. I thought we did a really good job in our end zone as far as making it difficult for them to get any sort of quality chances."

In the meantime, it was Fleury who held the fort. A stop on Blue Jackets defenseman Zach Werenski from point-blank range at 7:23, then using his catching glove to snare a Cam Atkinson attempt at 11:55.

Players insisted there was no fidgeting in the dressing room after they found out Murray was injured. They simply turned to the franchise's longest-tenured and easily its most loved player, and started filming an incredible sequel.

"What can you say about his character and his compete level, just to step in and be as good as he was, especially in that first period?" Sullivan wondered aloud about Fleury. "We needed him." ■

APRIL 14, 2017 · PITTSBURGH, PENNSYLVANIA
PENGUINS 4, BLUE JACKETS 1

Penguins Continue Mastery of Blue Jackets

Turning Their Other Cheek Paying Off

By Jason Mackey

Should the NHL decide to pivot and begin awarding goals based on hits delivered, the Penguins' first-round series against the Columbus Blue Jackets could take a decided turn.

Doubtful that happens, however.

Doesn't seem to be much of a precedent for that sort of seismic change, especially in the middle of the Stanley Cup playoffs.

Assuming there are no major rule alterations made within the next week or so, and assuming this sort of stuff keeps up, the Penguins' 4-1 victory in Game 2 at PPG Paints Arena has them staring at a sizable series edge while employing a strategy that's tough to stop.

Get timely goals and solid goaltending. Block shots. Protect your net. Forget the … stuff. Hard to argue with any of it, especially the last part given the rock 'em, sock 'em approach many Penguins expected from Columbus in this one.

"You don't win the game after the whistles," defenseman Ian Cole said. "You don't win the game in the scrums. You win the game between the whistles, and you win the game scoring goals and preventing goals.

"That's what we're going to continue to concentrate on. We've had a good, singular mindset here so far. We're going to try and continue to do that."

The Blue Jackets again tried to blast the Penguins to smithereens, accumulating a 51-30 edge in hits. The Penguins barely noticed, let alone retaliated. Not even when Matt Calvert snapped his stick by checking Tom Kuhnhackl from behind in the final minute.

The Blue Jackets certainly tried to ratchet up the offensive pressure, too, following coach John Tortorella's directive of doing a better job trying to pump shots through. The Penguins responded by blocking 23.

For those of you scoring at home, that's a hits advantage for Columbus of 101-65 through two games and 45 blocked shots for the Penguins, an average of 22.5 per game that's actually way, way better than their season mark (15.9).

"There's a sense of desperation in everything that we do in the playoffs," Cole said. "They've been trying to shoot a lot of pucks, which will inevitably lead to blocked shots. We're going to keep trying to be competitive and keep trying to get in shot lanes. If the blocked shots happen, that's great."

The same for stellar goaltending, which the

Marc-Andre Fleury denies the Blue Jackets in the first period of Game 2. Fleury would go on to stop 39 shots on the night. (Peter Diana/Post-Gazette)

Penguins got. Marc-Andre Fleury stopped 39 of 40 shots to earn his second win in the series and his 55th all-time in the postseason.

Another development two games into this series can explain the Penguins' first two goals. The line of Jake Guentzel, Sidney Crosby and Sheary was dynamic after a so-so performance in Game 1.

Sheary's forecheck forced Blue Jackets goaltender Sergei Bobrovsky into a turnover that led to Crosby's goal and a 1-0 lead. Crosby now has 50 playoff goals in his career, the 57th player in NHL history to reach that milestone.

After Saad beat Fleury from the left circle at 7:00 of the second period, Guentzel and Crosby executed a two-on-one break with precision, Guentzel using his quick release to score his sixth goal in seven games counting the regular season.

Malkin stretched the Penguins' lead to 3-1 at 2:01 of the third, scoring from a severe angle to give the Penguins some much-needed insurance before Patric Hornqvist tacked on an empty-netter late.

The Penguins will take the Malkin and Hornqvist tallies, but this night belonged to Sid and the Kids, driving possession and creative scoring chances nearly every time they hopped over the boards.

"When they're in that offensive zone, they're as dangerous a line as there is in the game right now," Penguins coach Mike Sullivan said.

The first two games of this series should tell you that the Penguins as a team are pretty darn dangerous, too. They don't get sucked into stupidity. They block shots like they get commission for each one. They appear dead set on clearing the crease for Fleury.

It's an airtight formula for winning playoff games.

"I think our discipline is important throughout this series," Sheary said. "In the playoffs, it can get a little heated.

"If we can stay away from that, we'll continue to be successful." ∎

APRIL 16, 2017 · COLUMBUS, OHIO
PENGUINS 5, BLUE JACKETS 4, OT

Sweep Is on Doorstep

Guentzel Caps Hat Trick in OT for a 3-0 Edge

By Jason Mackey

Penguins co-owner Mario Lemieux hooked a sharp right into the coaches' office that's adjacent to the Penguins dressing room here at Nationwide Arena and let out a throaty, celebratory scream.

The reason, of course, was a 5-4 overtime victory against the Columbus Blue Jackets, one that gave the Penguins a three-games-to-none grip on the series, one obtained by a team oozing resilience and an organization that employs some youngster named Jake who seems to have little regard for the whole idea of postseason experience.

That kid, Jake Guentzel, scored the overtime winner at 13:10 of the extra session, quickly sniping a feed from Sidney Crosby to complete his hat trick and finish the Penguins' comeback from a two-goal deficit after the first 20 minutes.

"The resilience and resolve this group shows is part of the fabric of our identity," Penguins coach Mike Sullivan said. "It has to be in order to have success in this league and win at this time of year."

So does a little luck and the occasional, fortuitous bounce. The Penguins had none of that sort of stuff in the first period. Only a bag full of bad puck luck.

Columbus forward Cam Atkinson scored 11 seconds into the game to put the Penguins in an early hole, then cashed in at 5:02 to make it 2-1. Blue Jackets defenseman Zach Werenski converted on the power play for their third goal and a 3-1 lead at 6:10 of the first.

In the dressing room at the first intermission, Nick Bonino said the Penguins talked about only one goal.

Basically to score one more of those than Columbus in the middle period.

"All we wanted to do was win the second period, whether it was by one or two goals," Bonino said. "We ended up being able to tie it. Coming into the third, we were pretty confident that we were in a good spot."

Bryan Rust and Evgeni Malkin scored in the second to make it 3-3, while Guentzel pushed the Penguins ahead for the first time at 11:48 of the third. Blue Jackets center Brandon Dubinsky forced overtime with his goal at 15:11 of the final period.

In Guentzel's past eight games dating to the regular season, he's been held without a goal once. Five of his past six games have been multi-point efforts. He has a total of nine goals in those eight games.

"[The playoffs] bring out everyone's best," Guentzel said. "It's fun to be a part of."

That seemed to be especially true of Bonino

Jake Guentzel (59) celebrates with Sidney Crosby after scoring the game-winner in overtime. (Peter Diana/Post-Gazette)

and Werenski. Bonino caught a puck with his jaw and returned. Phil Kessel's shot rode up Werenski's stick, cut him below the eye and forced him from the game for a bit.

But not — this was one of the biggest momentum swings in a game full of them — until after Rust had scored his second goal, with Werenski down and bloodied.

Werenski, easily the Blue Jackets' best player this series, returned for the third but couldn't go in overtime. The reason: He couldn't see.

Columbus coach John Tortorella touted Werenski's toughness.

"Doesn't surprise me with him," he said.

The Penguins aren't lacking for fortitude, either, a nugget you tend to pick up along the way to winning the Stanley Cup.

Which is why, down 3-1, the Penguins simply went to work.

"Not the start I or anybody wanted," said Marc-Andre Fleury, who stopped 33 of 37 shots but also served up a few more juicy rebounds than he would've liked. "I was pretty relaxed after that and still confident that we could come back in the game."

Malkin said he could sense that business was about to start booming with Rust's goal, a little bit of a fluke that fluttered through Sergei Bobrovsky's legs.

"Second goal, 3-2, it's close," Malkin said. "We had lots of time. We knew we were back. We started to play right — spend time in the offensive zone, play our game. Then we scored the third goal."

If the Penguins keep sticking to the game plan and continuing to flash this sort of resistance, there's likely going to be another reason to celebrate with the team's coaches here on Tuesday. ∎

Eastern Conference Quarterfinals, Game 4

APRIL 18, 2017 · COLUMBUS, OHIO
BLUE JACKETS 5, PENGUINS 4

Put the Brooms Away

Bad Starts Finally Catch Up to Penguins as They Blow Shot at Rare Sweep

By Jason Mackey

The Penguins finally got burned.

All series long, their starts against the Blue Jackets have lacked. Outshot by a lot in the first two. A two-goal deficit in Game 3, even though the Penguins insisted they liked their game.

There was pretty much nothing to like about their start in Game 4, a 5-4 Penguins loss at Nationwide Arena that kept them from sweeping Columbus out of the opening round.

The Penguins chased the game over the final 40 minutes, but the damage was done. There was no coming out of this one.

"You can't keep playing with fire like that," Matt Cullen said. "You have to have a better start. We know that.

"It's on us to respond here."

That opportunity will come in Game 5 at PPG Paints Arena. Should the Penguins have any hopes of clinching the series then, a better all-around game from the drop of the puck would be a wise thing to focus on.

"We weren't hard enough to play against," Penguins coach Mike Sullivan said. "It's hard to score your way through the playoffs. You've got to play the game the right way. You've got to defend. You have to make good decisions. You've got to

be hard to play against. I don't think we were as committed tonight as our team is accustomed to."

Give the Penguins this: They certainly said all the right things leading up to the game.

Insisted they needed to stay in the moment. No looking ahead.

Can't give Columbus life. Have to finish this thing in four.

Putting those words into action proved problematic.

"We knew they were going to come out hard and forecheck hard and create plays," Brian Dumoulin said. "They've done that. We have to match their urgency before Thursday."

The three goals were all different.

Blue Jackets defenseman Jack Johnson put Columbus ahead, 1-0, when his shot from above the right circle caromed off Sidney Crosby's skate.

Josh Anderson made it 2-0 at 18:56 when he cut down the right wing and pushed a shot past Marc-Andre Fleury.

Pine's Brandon Saad took the shot from above the right circle, and Markus Nutivaara swept it under Fleury for a 3-0 lead at 4:48 of the second period.

Columbus so far has shown great interest in beating the living daylights of the Penguins. In Game 4, they went another route.

Columbus Blue Jackets Markus Nutivaara, top left, Brandon Saad, bottom left, and Alexander Wennberg celebrate a goal in the second period of Game 4. (AP Images)

One of the reasons the Blue Jackets were able to grab momentum early was the damage they did off the rush. That hasn't happened often for the Penguins.

"We got beat a little bit in situations where we normally don't get beat," Ron Hainsey said. "We had a hard time getting the puck in and establishing much of a forecheck. It was a little more off the rush than it's been, to be honest with you. It wasn't so much getting grinded down on the forecheck. They had some chances off the rush. I think we gave up more there than we did the first three games."

The Penguins cut it to 3-2 on goals from Patric Hornqvist and Hainsey. The teams traded goals during a third period where the Penguins were forced to take a lot of chances.

The reason, of course, was a bad first 25 or so minutes.

"We weren't ready at the start," said Tom Kuhnhackl, who scored in the third to pull the Penguins within 4-3. "That haunted us until the end."

The good news is this shouldn't prove to be too terribly costly. The Penguins haven't given up a lot of chances off the rush.

Most teams also haven't shut down Jake Guentzel, Sidney Crosby and Conor Sheary the way the Blue Jackets did. Guentzel scored a shorthanded goal late, but Sullivan wasn't exactly complimentary of the trio postgame.

"I don't think they had the same jump that they normally have, for whatever reason," Sullivan said. "I think sometimes that happens in our game. Give Columbus credit. They played well."

From the start, too. Unlike the Penguins, who missed out on a chance to sweep a team for the first time since 2009 (Eastern Conference Final against Carolina).

"The start was not very good," Hainsey said. "The whole first, really, we got outplayed rather handily. Didn't create much. We got out of there with two. It could have been worse." ■

APRIL 20, 2017 · PITTSBURGH, PENNSYLVANIA
PENGUINS 5, BLUE JACKETS 2

Goodbye, Columbus

Rust Helps Penguins Deliver Knockout Blow, Advance to Round 2

By Jason Mackey

When the Penguins blew their chance at a sweep in Columbus, coach Mike Sullivan emphasized the need for everyone to reset their mindset.

Sullivan's team had to do that a few times in Game 5, but the Penguins ultimately got the result they desired, a 5-2 win over the Blue Jackets at PPG Paints Arena that pushed the Penguins through to the Eastern Conference semifinals.

It's that sort of ability, to assess and readjust on the fly, that separates the Penguins from most teams.

"Guys in the locker room have been there before," said Bryan Rust, the offensive hero on this night with a pair of goals, including the game-winner. "We've had elimination games that we haven't won. We just try to take each day as it comes. Each day is a new day. You can learn from the past game and move forward. I think we embraced the challenge and had fun with it."

A few of those veterans Rust alluded to stood tall in this one, too.

Literally.

After a lousy second period that saw them nearly fritter away a 3-0 lead, several Penguins leaders stood up in the dressing room and addressed the poor performance.

One that nearly brought with it another trip to Columbus.

"We needed to reset a little bit," Matt Cullen said. "You can carry that with you into the third period, then who knows where we end up?

"We didn't have a good second period. We were able to come in here. All of us knew we weren't happy with what had happened. We were able to sort of reset, step back, take a look at the situation and say, 'If we have our best period here, we're moving on.' I think as a group we did a good job of that."

In addition to Rust's two goals, Evgeni Malkin contributed three assists, and Marc-Andre Fleury stopped 49 of 51 shots to make this one happen.

Jake Guentzel led the Penguins in goals this series against the Blue Jackets with five, followed by Rust's four.

Malkin tallied 11 points in the five games, matching his career-high for points in a playoff series. He also had that many in six games against the New York Islanders in the 2013 Eastern Conference quarterfinals.

The biggest turning point in Game 5 came with a sequence early in the third period.

Columbus had what looked to be the game-tying goal wiped out because Alexander Wennberg made contact with Fleury and was called for goaltender interference.

Blue Jackets coach John Tortorella protested vehemently on the bench but afterward didn't feel

Bryan Rust just misses what would have been his third goal of the night during the third period of Pittsburgh's series-clinching win over Columbus in Game 5. (Peter Diana/Post-Gazette)

much like dissecting the play.

"You guys watched the game," Tortorella said. "You don't need my help with that."

A follow-up came on whether Tortorella thought Fleury was out of the crease when the contact occurred.

"I'm not talking about the play," Tortorella said. "Stop baiting me into it, please.

"There's no sense of me having a viewpoint on it. It happened."

On the ensuing power play, Sidney Crosby blasted a one-timer from the right circle to extend the Penguins' lead to 4-2 and allow them the opportunity to breathe.

"I think that's one of the things that makes our team as competitive as it is," Sullivan said. "These guys get big goals at key times that change outcomes."

And, of course, manage momentum swings, which the Penguins had to do early on.

Despite talking about wanting to have a better

start, the Penguins played the first five minutes like they wanted to see more of Columbus.

Thankfully for them, Fleury held the fort, denying Cam Atkinson from point-blank range, then making another stop on Wennberg.

Phil Kessel scored a power-play goal to flip the momentum in the Penguins' favor.

"Tonight was a big game," Kessel said. "You never want to go back there. Flower played real well. They're obviously a great team. It was a tough battle."

Sullivan felt the game was similar to this entire series: physical and back-and-forth, the need to handle such drastic swings heightened.

"I don't know that, in any moment in any game, that any one of us felt like we settled into the game, where it was more of a controlled game," Sullivan said. "It felt like it was an emotional rollercoaster."

One the Penguins were ultimately able to survive because of their experience taking these sorts of rides. ■

APRIL 27, 2017 · WASHINGTON, D.C.
PENGUINS 3, CAPITALS 2

Explosive Start, Big Finish

Bonino Scores Winner; Crosby Racks Up 2 Goals

By Jason Mackey

All the necessary traps were set for the Penguins to stumble. A long layoff. Playing the Washington Capitals. On the road. Instead, the Penguins came out of the gate strong, lagged a little in the middle and sprinted to the finish line.

A full week elapsed between games for the Penguins, long enough to screw with a team's mojo if it doesn't take practices seriously or long enough to correct a few flaws if it does.

Guess which route the Penguins took?

That seven-day break proved to be no big thing for the Penguins, perhaps even a good thing, as they took Game 1 of their Eastern Conference semifinal series against the Capitals, 3-2, at Verizon Center.

"We hadn't played for a little bit," said Penguins captain Sidney Crosby, who scored twice in 52 seconds to give the Penguins a 2-0 lead early in the second period. "We wanted to establish how we wanted to play. I thought we did a good job of that."

How rare was Thursday's Game 1 win?

- Despite winning eight of their nine previous playoff series against the Capitals, the Penguins had also dropped eight of their nine Game 1s against Washington, the lone exception a 7-0 win here in 2000.
- In their history, the Penguins entered this one

30-33 all-time in Game 1s, including a 7-18 mark on the road. Not exactly get-up-and-go sort of stuff.

- Although a 7-3-2 push late in the regular season helped, the Penguins' 19-15-7 road record was decidedly ordinary, a stark contrast from the 31-6-4 mark they posted at PPG Paints Arena.
- It was no different at this glow-stick-filled fun house, either, the Penguins ceding 12 goals and scoring three in a pair of lopsided losses.

Then again, the Penguins also have a bunch of big-game players, the kind who transform into something else come playoff time, and against the Capitals, Nick Bonino took his familiar spot at the front of the pack.

Bonino picked up the game-winning goal at 12:36 of the third period after Washington had erased a two-goal deficit. After ending this six-game series a season ago with an overtime goal, Bonino picked up right where he left off: torturing the Capitals.

Marc-Andre Fleury watched Bonino's heroics a season ago from the bench as Matt Murray's backup. This time around, he played a pivotal role, especially in the third period, flipping and flopping and stopping everything the Capitals threw at him.

When it ended, Fleury stopped 33 of 35 shots to pick up his 58th career postseason win,

Marc-Andre Fleury makes a crucial late stop against the Capitals during the third period of Game 1. (Peter Diana/Post-Gazette)

continuing to bring smiles to his teammates' faces with every additional memory created.

"That was him at his best right there," Matt Cullen said of Fleury's flurry. "He battles for us. It's been awesome the way he's played."

The groundwork the Penguins laid during their week of practice work was evident from the start of the game, an area that plagued them against the Blue Jackets when they were out-shot, 71-39, and out-scored, 5-3, in the opening 20 minutes.

Against the Capitals, the Penguins were outstanding defensively during the opening 20 minutes. Gaps were tight. They did a particularly fine job of denying passing lanes, several times knocking pucks out of their air with their sticks.

What impressed coach Mike Sullivan the most, however, was how quickly the Penguins exited their zone, a point of emphasis during several uptempo workouts at the UPMC Lemieux Sports Complex.

"The last week we've spent a lot of time on the ice and watching film, trying to come out of our zone a little bit cleaner," Sullivan said. "I thought our guys helped one another there. There was a lot to like in that first period."

And early in the second.

Crosby's first came off the opening faceoff. Former Penguin Matt Niskanen got caught in the neutral zone, and Jake Guentzel fed Crosby on a two-on-one break.

The second, at 1:04, featured a nifty past in the slot from Patric Hornqvist. Olli Maatta shot from well above the left circle. Capitals goaltender Braden Holtby fumbled the rebound, and Hornqvist made a quick, three-foot dish to Crosby, who came barreling in with speed.

Gifted every possible reason for a slow start to this series, the Penguins did nothing of the sort and instead got off on the right foot.

"It was pretty good," Crosby said of the first game back. "There's only so much you can do to prepare, but I thought we did a good job.

"We have to continue to get better here with every game, but it's good to get the first one." ■

APRIL 29, 2017 · WASHINGTON, D.C.
PENGUINS 6, CAPITALS 2

Penguins Dig Deep

Washington Has Shown Why It Was the Top Team, but It Is 0-2 in Series

By Jason Mackey

There's a definite difference here. It might be as big as the four-goal gulf that separated the teams who skated Saturday at Verizon Center, a 6-2 Penguins victory in Game 2 of their Eastern Conference semifinal that gave them a 2-0 lead in this series.

The Capitals are racking up shot attempts — 171 through two games — the way the Blue Jackets rang up hits. Same result, too. The Capitals outplayed the Penguins at the start and for stretches and look like darlings except when you turn your attention to the one stat that really matters — wins.

It's not all that dissimilar to when you take a bigger-picture look at these franchises, either.\

The Capitals have never won a Stanley Cup. They've been to one final. The Penguins, if they can figure out their starts, could become the first team to win back-to-back Cups since the Red Wings in 1997-98. With a 2-0 series lead, the thought of a ninth playoff series win in 10 tries against the Capitals is more than just smoke.

The Penguins haven't been perfect by any stretch, but they're flashing something these Capitals, despite winning the Presidents' Trophy, can't lay claim to — a proven track record of winning in the playoffs. Which often requires thriving in less-than-ideal circumstances.

"We were able to take advantage of a few chances tonight," coach Mike Sullivan said. "That helped us win the game. But what I love about our team is just their competitive spirit and finding ways to win. We had a few guys go down through the course of the game tonight. The bench, it's so great to listen to our players and how they support one another when they go over the boards. They're a privilege to coach. They play hard for one another. I think that's what makes our team what it is. I believe we have a unique chemistry. It's fun to be a part of it."

The players Sullivan mentioned were Patric Hornqvist, Tom Kuhnhackl and Ron Hainsey. All were hurt blocking shots. Sullivan did not have updates on any of them.

Another player who blocked a shot was Sidney Crosby. He tossed his body in front of a

Evgeni Malkin braces himself for a hit from Washington's T.J. Oshie during Game 2. Malkin contributed a goal and an assist as the Penguins won 6-2 to take a 2-0 series lead. (Peter Diana/Post-Gazette)

Justin Williams attempt, then poked the puck the other way, leading to a 2-on-1 rush and a Jake Guentzel goal.

Sullivan talks often about resilience. Coming back from the abyss that was the Penguins first period in this one was more than that.

The Penguins were getting outshot, 23-6, and out-attempted, 48-11, at one point. It may not have been that close.

But then Crosby gathered a puck between his legs and zipped a pinpoint pass to Phil Kessel, who whipped a shot past Braden Holtby. This followed 40-year-old Matt Cullen winning a footrace with trade deadline darling Kevin Shattenkirk and scoring a short-handed goal.

The Penguins mustered just 45 shot attempts, giving them 86 in two games — or two fewer than the Capitals on this night.

It hardly mattered.

"It makes us a dangerous team," goalie Marc-Andre Fleury said. "We don't need to generate that many shots and still get good scoring chances."

The Penguins are also a dangerous team because of how well Fleury has played in goal. He stopped 34 of 36 Capitals shots, kept the Penguins in it early and continued to author one magical story this postseason. In seven games, Fleury has a 2.37 goals-against average and a .936 save percentage.

"He's been our best player," Sullivan said. "In the first series, in the first two games here, he's made timely saves for us, especially in that first period. I don't know what else I can say. He's a great competitor. He's a great teammate. And he's really risen to the challenge."

The Capitals are in a dangerous position.

Of the 87 times an NHL team has lost the first two games of a playoff at home, only 18 have come back to win the series, a mere 21 percent. The Penguins also went 31-6-4 on home ice in the regular season and have won all three playoff games played there this season.

Game 3 is Monday at PPG Paints Arena.

Whether they'll have Hainsey appears iffy. He took an Alex Ovechkin one-timer to the back/side of his head in the third period.

Hornqvist was felled by a John Carlson slapper in the first. Kuhnhackl was sporting an ice bag on his wrist after and looked fine.

Without Hornqvist, one of their biggest battlers, the Penguins changed nothing. They awoke from another sleepy start and chased Holtby with three goals on 14 shots.

They did it, too, on minimal chances.

"You look at tonight, it wasn't a situation where you had chance after chance after chance," Crosby said. "We got some good looks, and we put them in. It's not always going to work like that, but you have to be able to win different ways. Tonight, with the start we had, we needed to be able to find a way to grab momentum back."

And that's the difference between these teams, one that has not yet figured out how to break through when times are tough. Another that does it with regularity.

"We have a gritty group," Sullivan said. "They're scrappy. It's a never-say-die attitude. It's not perfect by any stretch out there, and we're aware of that. We know that. What I love about this group of players is that they respond the right way. They've shown an ability to do that time and time again. This group finds ways to have success." ■

Matt Cullen celebrates after scoring a short-handed goal in the second period to give the Penguins a 1-0 lead. (Peter Diana/Post-Gazette)

Eastern Conference Semifinals, Game 3

MAY 1, 2017 · PITTSBURGH, PENNSYLVANIA
CAPITALS 3, PENGUINS 2, OT

This One Hurts

Crosby Injured in First Period; Status Uncertain

By Jason Mackey

Penguins captain Sidney Crosby was injured Monday.

How severe? Uncertain at this point. The same for whether it's one injury or two or how long Crosby could potentially be out.

What we do know is this: The Penguins' Eastern Conference semifinal series against the Capitals has changed, the only thing that's to be determined is by how much.

Capitals defenseman Kevin Shattenkirk scored at 3:13 of overtime to produce a 3-2 Capitals win in Game 3 at PPG Paints Arena.

Had a Penguins player scored, a sweep would've seemed plausible. Now, the Capitals have life. Can the Penguins counter that with the return of their captain? We shall see.

"We showed for parts of 50 minutes that we can play them without Sid," Nick Bonino said. "Obviously we want him here, but if he's not, we have to find ways to win. We almost did tonight."

Crosby was injured at 5:24 of the opening period and did not return. Penguins coach Mike Sullivan had no update afterward. He also declined to say whether it was one or two issues Crosby was dealing with and, per Sullivan's usual, he declined to levy an opinion.

"I'd rather not share my opinion," Sullivan said.

Alex Ovechkin made initial contact with Crosby, his stick coming up high. It also appeared that Ovechkin used his legs to knock Crosby off balance. With Crosby unable to avoid contact or protect himself, former Penguin Matt Niskanen cross-checked him in the head. Crosby's left leg was pinned underneath him, and it shot out violently and awkwardly as he hit the ice.

Crosby remained face-down on the ice for nearly a minute before standing and leaving the ice with help from head athletic trainer Chris Stewart.

Niskanen was given a five-minute major for cross-checking, which carries with it an automatic game misconduct.

"I like Nisky as a person," Chris Kunitz said. "I don't think it's a very nice hit. I don't think it's something this game is looking for, especially against someone who means so much to our team."

If the Penguins are without Crosby for any length of time, Jake Guentzel, Evgeni Malkin and Phil Kessel will have to carry an even heavier offensive load.

Guentzel has drawn statistical comparisons to Maurice "Rocket" Richard. Only one player — San Jose's Joe Pavelski — has scored more than Phil Kessel's 14 goals since the start of last postseason. Malkin remains the postseason scoring leader and tallied at 18:07 of the third to ignite the Penguins' comeback from a 2-0 deficit to force overtime.

"Everyone stepped up," Guentzel said. "A player like Sid, obviously it affects everyone. Just got to find a way."

Sidney Crosby is helped to his feet by trainer Chris Stewart in the first period of Game 3 against the Capitals at PPG Paints Arena. (Peter Diana/Post-Gazette)

Marc-Andre Fleury does not score goals, although he'd certainly like to one day.

His role becomes even more important with Crosby out.

Fleury had posted a .951 save percentage and a 2.00 goals-against average while winning his past three starts and was spectacular at times Monday, despite allowing three goals on 33 shots.

The Capitals first goal — credited to Nicklas Backstrom — wasn't Fleury's fault; it bounced off Ian Cole. The second was a defensive breakdown. Even Shattenkirk's point shot was iffy.

The Penguins also have a strong playoff history against Washington, winning eight of nine series against them. Furthermore, they're 15-2 all-time when taking a 2-0 lead in a series, 8-0 during the Crosby-Malkin Era.

"This game's over," Trevor Daley said. "Try to forget about it. We still have a chance to put ourselves in a good situation. We have to come out hard next one."

And also perhaps tighten up their penalty kill. The Capitals scored a pair of power-play goals Monday, a weapon for Washington the Penguins do not want to introduce in this battle, one that's growing more physical by the minute.

The Penguins will also have to hope for good news on Conor Sheary, who collided with Patric Hornqvist at 2:24 of the second period and did not return. Sheary, however, was spotted in the building looking no worse for wear.

So, let the debate over the legality of Niskanen's hit rage on. Capitals coach Barry Trotz called it a hockey play, then got feisty with a reporter who asked whether Ovechkin's role was also a hockey play.

Doesn't matter.

What matters most for the Penguins is resetting, refocusing and hoping for the best for their best in Crosby.

"We're hopeful, first of all, that won't be the case," Sullivan said of potentially missing Crosby. "I think this group has so much character and talent that we're able to endure the injuries that we have. We've done it all year long. We did it again tonight. We'll continue to do it.

"We knew this was going to be a hard series. Washington is a very good hockey team. It's nothing that we didn't expect. We'll reset our mindset. We'll get our rest and be ready for Game 4." ▪

Eastern Conference Semifinals, Game 4

MAY 3, 2017 · PITTSBURGH, PENNSYLVANIA
PENGUINS 3, CAPITALS 2

Just a Hockey Win

Even Without Crosby, Penguins Find Ways to Seize 3-1 Series Lead

By Jason Mackey

The same message was repeated at every stall inside the Penguins dressing room from the moment it was announced that captain Sidney Crosby had a concussion and would be out for an undetermined amount of time.

We've been through this all year, Penguins players reminded pretty much anyone within earshot. There are capable people here. Plenty of offensive talent, too. Focus on Game 4. Look forward. No excuses. Just play.

The Penguins put that mindset — drilled into them daily by coach Mike Sullivan — into practice Wednesday during a 3-2 win over the Capitals in Game 4 of the Eastern Conference semifinals at PPG Paints Arena.

"We knew we had the guys in this room to get the job done," said Justin Schultz, whose power-play bomb at 11:24 of the second period stood up as the game-winner. "Obviously Sid is a big part of this team. We miss him out there. But we have the guys in here who can step up, and we showed it [Wednesday]."

In the process, the Penguins grabbed a 3-1 advantage in the series.

Funny thing about the Penguins leadership group: With Crosby out, it's not as though one man — perhaps Evgeni Malkin, Chris Kunitz or Matt Cullen — delivered some sort of impromptu sermon. It's not their style.

There was simply a quiet realization of what needed to be done. And without the best player in the NHL, winning performances would have to come from other sources, by whatever means possible.

Patric Hornqvist, one of the few vocal leaders the Penguins do have, scored the first goal and gave the building a jolt of life. He also played through an injury, the result of catching another shot in a bad spot.

Marc-Andre Fleury continued to stand on his head, stopping 36 of 38 shots. And the Penguins blocked 24 Capitals shot attempts in what Olli Maatta called a "battle win."

"We don't have a lot of guys who are too vocal," Kunitz said. "Guys try to let their performance dictate how we talk as a team."

Washington's Matt Niskanen cross-checks Bryan Rust during Game 4. Despite playing without Sidney Crosby, the Penguins won Game 4 to take a 3-1 series lead. (Peter Diana/Post-Gazette)

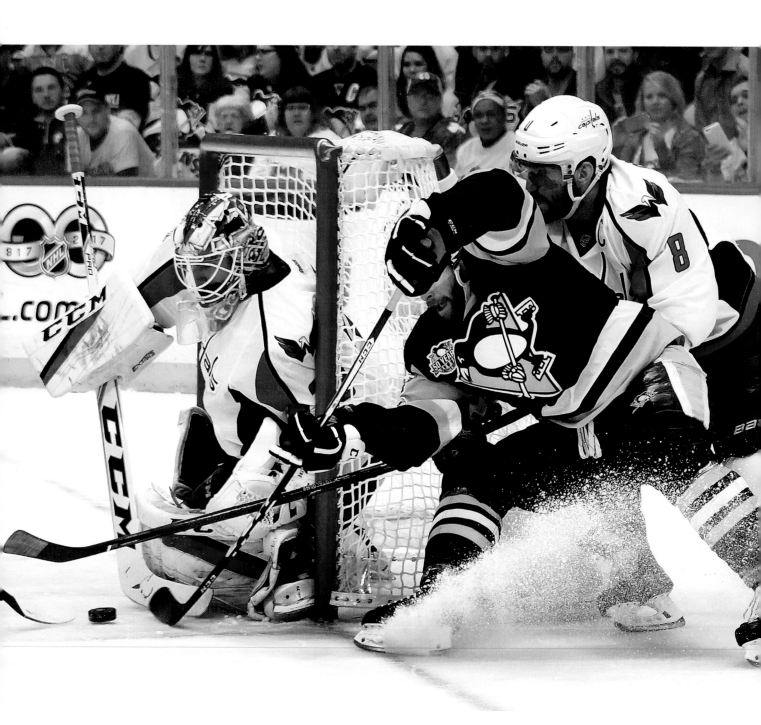

Bryan Rust tries to wrap the puck around the net on Capitals goalie Braden Holtby. The Penguins' 18 shots on goal proved enough as Pittsburgh won Game 4 by a 3-2 score. (Peter Diana/Post-Gazette)

The Penguins said plenty with this win, even if it wasn't exactly perfect.

"You hopped on the ice, and you didn't worry about anything else," Maatta said. "You went out there, you played. We battled really hard."

The situation in which the Penguins' seriousness showed up should matter. Lose Wednesday and go back to Washington tied at two games apiece, that's a bad recipe. The Capitals have the momentum, back in their building.

Instead, the Penguins stamped out any hope. They're 15-2 when jumping ahead, 2-0, in a series.

Washington had a 38-18 advantage in shots on goal and dictated terms for long stretches late. The difference was that their goaltender, Braden Holtby, has underperformed for much of this series, while Fleury is on another planet right now.

"Marc is a guy who elevated the team at the most important time of the season," Sullivan said.

"I think we all know how good he is," Maatta added. "He's really showing it these playoffs. He's been awesome. Probably our best player."

Hornqvist scored at 4:39 of the first, on a breakaway, something he rarely enjoys. Jake Guentzel stretched the lead to 2-0 at 3:51 of the second when his harmless shot kicked off Dmitry Orlov's skate.

Evgeny Kuznetsov and Nate Schmidt brought the Capitals back even with goals 72 seconds apart in the second.

With John Carlson off for roughing, Schultz stepped into a one-time feed from Malkin, a swing that would have made David Ortiz proud.

"I knew I got all of it," Schultz said. "I didn't know it was going in."

The Penguins finished 1 for 5 on the power play, that unit getting a bunch of time because the Capitals kept taking offensive-zone penalties. Washington failed to score on its four power-play chances.

An especially crucial special teams moment unfolded at 18:00 of the second period. Cullen was handed a double minor for high-sticking, and the infraction carried over to the third period.

Another big penalty kill. More blocked shots. A gritty performance that wasn't necessarily the skill and flash of Crosby but, more important, the willingness to do whatever it takes to win.

And the Penguins protecting a third period lead — they're 76-1-1 the past two years in that situation — by any means necessary, a testament to what's understood with this group.

"We've been doing it the whole year," Hornqvist said. "Sid is a big loss for us. We went and got that win for him. We all played really, really hard. We didn't play our best game, but we found a way to win. That's all that matters in the end."

MAY 6, 2017 · WASHINGTON, D.C.
CAPITALS 4, PENGUINS 2

Capitals Find Late Life

Lead Slips away from Penguins in Third Period to Draw Series to 3-2

By Jason Mackey

Protecting third-period leads has become a staple for coach Mike Sullivan's teams. They entered Saturday's Game 5 against the Capitals winners of 94 of their past 98 games — regular season and playoffs — when leading after two periods before things went awry on this night.

Or, as Nick Bonino said, "It kind of all went to pieces for us."

The Capitals scored three times in the third en route to a 4-2 win that extends the Eastern Conference semifinals to a sixth game back in Pittsburgh.

It wasn't the Penguins best, but the general takeaway was that these were extremely correctable mistakes.

"It's tough," Bonino said. "It's a good team. They get a goal. On the bench, the whole team kind of maybe got a little bit worried. I'm not sure what it is. I can't explain it. For about 5-10 minutes there, we didn't play well. They capitalized. That's one of the best teams in the league. They'll do that to you."

Nicklas Backstrom, Evgeny Kuznetsov and Alex Ovechkin struck in the final 20 minutes for Washington, two of them in a 27-second span, as the Capitals staved off elimination against a team that has beaten them in eight of nine playoff meetings all-time.

The Backstrom goal was the real backbreaker, the one that got the ball rolling.

Washington attacked with far too much ease, a theme for parts of this night. With Backstrom in the left circle, Marc-Andre Fleury had a clean look but couldn't stop it.

"They kept coming at us," Fleury said. "They put the puck on net. Some that I would like to have back. That's what happens."

Until that Backstrom goal, the Penguins actually attacked quite a bit, the mentality that had staked them to a 2-1 lead in the first place. Then, things changed.

"I thought that goal was avoidable," Sullivan said. "We gave them life. Give them credit. They have good players. They scored a couple of key goals to get them back in the game. I think a lot of the third period, we had some pushback. We had

Capitals goaltender Braden Holtby stops a shot in the third period. Holtby had 20 saves in Washington's 4-2 win. (Matt Freed/Post-Gazette)

some opportunities. We had some real high-quality chances. We didn't convert."

The Penguins did convert early. Carl Hagelin picked up one in the first — off a slick, no-look feed from Bonino — while Phil Kessel completed a pretty sequence of power-play passing in the second period.

But that was it.

Evgeny Kuznetsov threw a bad-angle shot at Fleury that snuck through, and Ovechkin followed his own rebound and roofed it for the final margin.

Both were scored off blocked shots, something the Penguins have racked up at a crazy pace this series, including 20 on Saturday. That alone tells the razor-thin tale, the unpredictability of a bouncing puck.

Sullivan recognized that but wasn't ready to put too much stock into one night.

"If you're watching the other games that are going on right now, there are a lot of goals that are scored like that," Sullivan said. "Teams defend hard. The teams that are left, they're good teams at both ends of the rink. It's hard to get to the scoring area because teams defend so hard. We're not going to overthink it. We did a lot of good things tonight. It's two pretty good hockey teams that are playing against one another. We've got to have a short memory. We have to go home, reset our mindset and try to put our very best on the ice."

Game 5 also featured three excellent players all performing their best. It hasn't happened a ton for Washington in this series.

And that doesn't take into account goaltender Braden Holtby, who was likely the Capitals' best player in stopping 20 of 22 shots. He was certainly better than Fleury, who allowed four goals on 32 shots.

Yet nobody inside the Penguins seemed all that up in arms. Sure, they stubbed their toe on a chance to convert a series-clinching kick, but nothing that transpired here torpedoed their belief that this is a perfectly winnable series.

"They made the most of that momentum swing," Hagelin said. "They took this win. Our focus is on the next game."

The Penguins' focus will be continuing to look good on the power play, which certainly happened. It will also be continuing to rely on Sidney Crosby; he returned from a one-game absence from a concussion and picked up right where he left off with an assist.

Evgeni Malkin, too, recorded a helper to stretch his NHL lead in playoff points to 17 in 10 games.

The Penguins have a challenge ahead of them. Their defenseman need to tighten a few gaps, and everybody could stand to play with the puck a bit more.

"We're spending a little too much time in our zone," Bonino said. "I think we can end plays sooner. They're not getting just one shot. They're retrieving pucks, they're retrieving all the rebounds and getting them back to the net. If we can make them one-and done, maybe that would help us."

Freaking out over one loss would not.

Especially against a team they historically own in the playoffs.

And it seems like the Penguins are keenly aware that they still have another gear to reach.

"It's a good team down there," Olli Maatta said. "It's not going to be easy. We knew that coming into the games. At the same time, I don't think we played our best game. I don't think we've shown our best yet." ■

Washington's Tom Wilson celebrates after Alex Ovechkin's goal in the third period gave the Capitals a 4-2 lead in Game 5. (Matt Freed/Post-Gazette)

MAY 8, 2017 · PITTSBURGH, PENNSYLVANIA
CAPITALS 5, PENGUINS 2

One Loss After Another

But Malkin Guarantees Game 7 Win

By Jason Mackey

Spend hours analyzing Monday's 5-2 Penguins loss whichever way you want — video, analytics, eye test, doesn't matter. The Capitals basically played 60 minutes of Whack-A-Munch against the Penguins in Game 6 of the Eastern Conference semifinals and won a boatload of tickets.

Evgeni Malkin doesn't care. Washington may have the momentum in this series, but Malkin matched that with a guarantee following one of the more wretched playoff performances in franchise history.

"They think they won an easy game tonight," Malkin said. "They think they can win Game 7. I say, 'No.'

"We have a great team. I believe in my team. We need to understand that we've been in Game 7 before. We need to play the same. First period is really important. Be ready."

Malkin would know what it's going to take to steer this ship in the opposite direction.

In 2009, in this round, the Penguins had to go back to D.C. and clinch — and obviously did.

In his postgame comments, Malkin repeatedly said the Penguins had to support one another and also have a little fun in Game 7.

"Tough game for us," Malkin said. "We need to forget this game. It's bad luck for us tonight. Nothing worked. No power play, no penalty kill, no five-on-five.

"But we know we have a good team. We know we have a good goalie. If we play how we can, 100 percent, we can win."

Whatever transpired on PPG Paints Arena ice Monday was less than 100 percent. Maybe less than 10.

The Penguins tallied three shots on goal in the first period, and one of them was actually a 136-foot clear by Brian Dumoulin. They had eight after two periods.

Same as they have for much of this series, the Penguins struggled to quickly and effectively exit their own zone. They also struggled to make smart decisions with the puck, a confluence of events that turned ugly with three goals in 5:21 during the third period that turned this one into a rout.

"We're spending a lot of time on our half of the ice," Ron Hainsey said. "We're spending so much time on our half of the ice that eventually some things are going to happen."

One of the only positives to take out of this game — other than Jake Guentzel and Malkin smearing some lipstick on the pig with late goals — was the fact that Sidney Crosby is

Capitals winger T.J. Oshie scores in the first period of Game 6, part of a 5-2 beating the Penguins would have to rebound from in Game 7. (Matt Freed/Post-Gazette)

not again concussed.

He crashed hard into the boards late in the first period. It was not a dirty play, but it was ugly. Especially as Crosby seemed to stagger to his skates, continue play and taking another shift before the first period.

Coach Mike Sullivan said Crosby was not evaluated for a concussion at the first intermission.

Sullivan's answer on Crosby was a simple "no" that also covered whether he was worried Crosby may have been concussed.

Terse? Yes. But certainly not out of bounds given what Sullivan watched transpire and knows he has to correct before Wednesday.

Not only the own-zone play, a drum Sullivan has been banging this whole series, but also the Penguins' decision-making. That has stymied any semblance of offensive-zone time and obliterated their chance at sustained pressure.

Malkin said the Penguins made it entirely too

easy on the Capitals, and he's not wrong.

Nicklas Backstrom toyed with the Penguins penalty kill, pulling the defensive pressure to him setting up T.J. Oshie's power-play goal in the first.

Andre Burakovsky hit Hainsey and stripped the puck away from him for a 2-0 lead.

Backstrom's goal was one of several two-on-one rushes.

John Carlson scored on a shot from Monroeville, and Burakovsky freely cut into the slot and scored for No. 5.

"This league is going to test your resilience," Sullivan said. "It's going to test your resolve. You have to find ways to re-energize, and we can't let this one affect us."

"Nobody feels good about our game tonight," Crosby added. "We can talk about it all we want as far as not playing the way we need to to win games. I think it's more about what we need to do to win the next one." ■

Eastern Conference Semifinals, Game 7

MAY 10, 2017 · WASHINGTON, D.C.
PENGUINS 2, CAPITALS 0

Knockout Punch

Rust (Who Else?) Scores Winner; Fleury Slams Door on Capitals

By Jason Mackey

One was a Detroit Red Wings fan at the time and a newly licensed driver. The other was an established NHL player, a franchise goalie and the guy who thwarted an Alex Ovechkin breakaway to put on tape a highlight that would be replayed for years to come.

Despite coming at this one-sided rivalry from vastly different angles, Bryan Rust and Marc-Andre Fleury combined to torture the Washington Capitals once again.

Rust scored the game-winning goal in the second period, Fleury stopped all 29 shots he faced, and the Penguins left Verizon Center with a 2-0 win in Game 7 and a trip to the Eastern Conference final ahead.

"It's been fun," Fleury said. "It's tiring. It's a long series. They're a good team. They came hard at us until the end. We're proud of the way we played tonight and the way we handled the pressure."

Few are more qualified to speak on handling adverse circumstances than Fleury, who had his job taken by a kid in Matt Murray, then was thrust into duty just minutes before the start of the playoffs when Murray got hurt.

And on this night, when Murray dressed as his backup — a not-so-subtle reminder that the clock could strike midnight at any time — Fleury did not let this Cinderella story end.

Instead, he pushed the Penguins on to the next round, turning the Capitals into the Penguins' version of the Washington Generals.

"Flower's been our best player the whole playoffs," said Patric Hornqvist, who added a key insurance goal in the third.

Now, the Penguins will host the Ottawa Senators in the third round of the Stanley Cup playoffs.

The Penguins and Capitals have now met 10 times in the postseason. The Penguins have won nine times, including that 2009 Eastern Conference semifinal that Fleury helped win and Rust only casually watched, too consumed by what Detroit was doing.

The Capitals, who haven't been past this point since 1998, have now lost seven of 10 Game 7s during the Ovechkin Era.

Penguins Ian Cole and Sidney Crosby congratulate Bryan Rust after scoring on Capitals goaltender Braden Holtby in the second period of Game 7 of the Eastern Conference semifinals. (Matt Freed/Post-Gazette)

The Penguins, meanwhile, improved to 6-0 in Game 7s on the road and 4-0 all-time in Game 7s against Washington.

Count Rust and Fleury among the reasons, but don't forget a lock-down third period, when the Penguins allowed just six shots on goal.

And make sure to remember a few tactical adjustments coach Mike Sullivan made at practice.

Defensemen jumped into the play with greater urgency. Breakouts improved. The Penguins rolled those two things, alone with a better speed game, into sustained offensive pressure.

"Nobody was happy with how we played at home there in front of our fans in Game 6," Hornqvist said. "They were all over us like we were in the third period to them.

"I think we played a really strong game, but in the third we really took over."

So many highlights in this one, but the one you'll see the most transpired at 16:08 of the third period. Fleury stoned Ovechkin on a one-time attempt from the slot with the shaft of his stick.

Afterward, Fleury flashed his signature grin, the smile poking through his mask, as he rubbed the shaft of his stick.

"I didn't see [Ovechkin]," Fleury recalled. "When [Tom Wilson] made the pass, I just tried to get across as quick as possible, get something there. Fortunately enough to get a little piece."

And then had a conversation with his stick.

"I said, 'Thank you. Good job,'" Fleury said.

That stick wasn't alone on this night in terms of good jobs done, as the Penguins cracked the ruler across the Capitals' knuckles once more.

Little plays from the defense salvaged a series that was hardly the group's best.

Things like Ian Cole's keep-in on Rust's goal, a one-timer snipe where Jake Guentzel flashed a ton of poise and patience with the puck. Also Justin Schultz stepping up on Ovechkin to cause the turnover that led to Hornqvist's tally.

A few days ago, the Penguins defensemen either weren't trying such things or, when they did, they were toast.

"We're a team that learns from its mistakes," Brian Dumoulin said. "We know that, as a team, we can't sit back. That's not our game. I thought the guys did a great job of getting sticks on pucks and disrupting."

Nobody disrupted what was supposed to be a cathartic scene in Washington more than Fleury, who's doing his darnedest to shake past criticisms of how he's performed in the playoffs.

And he was joined by Rust, who shouldered his way into this rivalry in a Big Goal Bryan sort of way, scoring in yet another elimination game.

"Guys are happy in here," said Rust, who now has eight goals and nine points in 12 elimination games. "It shows our resilience and our ability to put the bad things behind us. Despite the good or the bad, we just have to keep playing." ∎

Scott Wilson fights Capitals defenseman Brooks Orpik in the third period of the Penguins' series-clinching Game 7 win over their rivals. (Matt Freed/Post-Gazette)

Eastern Conference Final, Game 1

MAY 13, 2017 · PITTSBURGH, PENNSYLVANIA
SENATORS 2, PENGUINS 1, OT

Ottawa Wins OT Opener

Senators Goalie Excels, Makes 27 Saves in Big Victory

By Jason Mackey

There's a cheat code when confronting the Ottawa Senators' choke hold of a defensive system.

They can clog up the neutral zone all they want with their 1-3-1 alignment on five-on-five play, but it becomes mathematically impossible — not to mention illegal — to do the same stuff while killing a penalty.

The Penguins were gifted an opportunity to make a difference with their power play in Game 1 of the Eastern Conference final at PPG Paints Arena. Several of them, as a matter of fact.

But that unit, ranked third in the NHL in the regular season, did not come through, and it allowed the Senators to escape with a 2-1 overtime victory.

"We need to help the team score," Evgeni Malkin said. "Our power play is usually so much better."

What made Game 1 especially frustrating was that the Penguins had five chances spread over 8:39. They fired 10 shots on goal, but none of them snuck past Senators goaltender Craig Anderson, who stopped 27 of 28 shots and turned out to be the difference-maker. Five minutes and 50 seconds of that chunk of power-play time came in the opening period.

"Our power play had the opportunity to be the difference in the first period," Penguins coach Mike Sullivan said. "We didn't execute."

Should the Penguins score at least one goal in ample power-play time, who knows what happens? It's infinitely easier to navigate a shutdown system when ahead, especially when you're talking about a team such as Ottawa that isn't exactly known for prolific offense.

The issue Game 1 was too much perimeter passing, Malkin said. For Game 2, they need to use Sidney Crosby and Patric Hornqvist down low more.

This is not new, either. When the Penguins power play struggles, it's often because of overpassing or not simplifying.

Over the past six games, the Penguins power play has scored twice on 22 chances.

That's not close to good enough for the amount of talent the Penguins have on their top unit.

Going 0 for 5 would be frustrating any day of the week, but it hurt more Saturday because the Penguins actually did a pretty good job of managing Ottawa's 1-3-1.

"I don't think the neutral zone was the issue," Sullivan said.

Friday at practice, Sullivan and his staff

Marc-Andre Fleury makes a stick-save on the Senators' Derick Brassard in the opening game of the Eastern Conference final. (Matt Freed/Post-Gazette)

emphasized a careful approach through the neutral zone, and that mostly paid off.

Problem was, other key parts of their game wound up stuck in neutral, the power play chief among them.

Most egregious for the Penguins power play was a five-on-three advantage in the first period. With the top unit on the ice, the Penguins struggled to enter the offensive zone cleanly, let alone score.

Ottawa took a 1-0 lead at 14:32 of the second period after a Penguins defensive gaffe. Brian Dumoulin turned it over behind his net. Bobby Ryan slid a backhand, no-look pass out to Jean-Gabriel Pageau, who scored his eighth goal of the playoffs from the inner-edge of the right circle.

Their best offensive chance via the power play came with Mark Stone off for interference midway through the second period. Hornqvist got his stick on a Justin Schultz point shot. The puck caromed off Dion Phaneuf's skate in the slot, but Anderson,

despite moving the other way, gloved it.

"It's nothing we haven't seen before," Schultz said of the Senators penalty-kill. "We just have to execute. We didn't tonight."

Malkin tied the score and forced overtime with his goal at 14:25 of the third period, as he deflected a Chris Kunitz feed from the right circle.

In overtime, Ryan tapped a puck out of a scrum and past Bryan Rust, as he used his speed and roofed a shot past Fleury. Sullivan called both goals "preventable."

If the Penguins could have gotten any semblance of a result with their power play, however, the quality of the Senators' goal would have hardly mattered.

"We didn't score five-on-three, five-on-four," Malkin said. "We started to get frustrated. We're mad at each other a little bit. We need to forget everything. It's the conference final. Sometimes it's not working. We need to support each other next game." ■

MAY 15, 2017 · PITTSBURGH, PENNSYLVANIA
PENGUINS 1, SENATORS 0

Once Is Enough

Kessel Scores; Fleury Shuts Out Senators

By Jason Mackey

Head athletic trainer Chris Stewart approached Penguins coach Mike Sullivan, covered his mouth with a towel and appeared to deliver some bad news.

It was the same message that Sullivan has to be tired of hearing by now: Defenseman Justin Schultz and forward Bryan Rust would remain out after suffering injuries in the first period of Game 2 against the Ottawa Senators in the Eastern Conference final.

Accustomed to playing shorthanded for much of the second half of the regular season, however, the Penguins didn't blink. They simply pressed on and dug themselves out of a series deficit, another familiar refrain for Sullivan's group.

After the Penguins tilted the ice in their favor during the second half of the game, Phil Kessel scored the only goal the Penguins would need midway through the third period to produce a 1-0 victory, evening the series at one game apiece.

"We're a pretty resilient group," Kessel said. "We've been there before. We have guys who can step in and step up. We found a way to get it done tonight."

That the Penguins were in position to get Kessel's goal at 13:05 of the final period served as a testament to their resilience and never-say-die attitude. Down to 16 skaters, the Penguins willed their way to a win, taking over the game completely in the third period.

"I was impressed with the way that we handled it," Matt Cullen said. "Obviously it's not ideal when you lose a couple guys like that who are so important. I was impressed with the way that the guys handled it. Our resilience paid off tonight."

On Kessel's goal, too. After Jean-Gabriel Pageau blocked the first attempt, Kessel got his own rebound and scored.

"Lucky bounce," Kessel said. "It got blocked. I got it off quick. It went in."

Kessel's goal was the culmination of an emotional effort from him. Not long before he beat Senators goaltender Craig Anderson for his sixth goal of the playoffs, Kessel could be seen yelling and gesturing wildly on the bench.

"To be honest, I think I yelled more than once tonight," Kessel said. "I don't remember that time."

Kessel's teammates did, however.

"I don't know that that's anything really out of

Phil Kessel (81) is congratulated by Chris Kunitz (14) after scoring the game-winning goal against the Senators in the third period of Game 2. (Matt Freed/Post-Gazette)

the ordinary," Cullen said. "It's kind of funny. Sometimes that just brings out the best in him. He's got that fire under there. He doesn't always show it."

"I missed the show," Marc-Andre Fleury added. "I'll have to watch the replay on that. When Phil is emotional, he's into it. He's a threat out there. Again tonight, he came up big for us."

So did the Penguins defensemen, so accustomed to playing a man down.

Brian Dumoulin logged a game-high 26:08, while Olli Maatta took over as quarterback of the top power play and picked up an assist on Kessel's goal.

"I thought they did a great job," Sullivan said of his defensemen. "We believe we have a defense corps that have the ability to spread the minutes."

No updates were available on Schultz or Rust. Couple their exits with the fact that Patric Hornqvist was an unexpected, late scratch, presumably due to injury, and the end result could cause concern when looking beyond Game 2.

The Penguins took a decided advantage in offense created and work ethic during the second period, turning the game's momentum in their favor, but they were unable to get a tangible reward for any of that.

All they had to show was a 20-16 lead in shots on goal after two, a 12-6 advantage in the second period alone and 43-22 lead when it came to attempted shots during the first 40 minutes.

In the third period, Anderson made a pair of terrific stops, first on Chad Ruhwedel from the right circle, another on Guentzel from in front. Anderson has been helped by the Penguins pinging posts and the crossbar.

Anderson stopped 28 of 29 shots, but he was one goal worse than Fleury, who recorded his second shutout in the past three games by making 23 stops.

Senators defenseman Dion Phaneuf plastered Rust with an elbow to the head, while Schultz barreled shoulder first into the end boards following a hit from Mike Hoffman.

Nevertheless, the Penguins pressed on.

"It's hockey," Sullivan said. "What I love about this group of players is we can win different ways." ∎

Penguins goaltender Marc-Andre Fleury makes a save on Senators forward Zack Smith in the first period of Game 2 of the Eastern Conference final. (Matt Freed/Post-Gazette)

MAY 17, 2017 · OTTAWA, ONTARIO
SENATORS 5, PENGUINS 1

Rotten Night at the Office

Ottawa Storms to Fast, 4-0 Lead, Drives Fleury Out With Onslaught

By Jason Mackey

Marc-Andre Fleury played the part of easy target after the Penguins' 5-1 loss to the Senators in Game 3 of the Eastern Conference final at Canadian Tire Centre, allowing four goals on the first nine shots he faced.

Accurate? Yeah, right. Just ask Matt Cullen, who was fairly steaming after this one.

"We played like [expletive]," Cullen said. "No excuses. That's the bottom line. We didn't battle. We didn't work as hard as we needed to. It's the conference finals. To have that kind of effort is pretty tough to stomach."

The effort Cullen mentioned prohibited the Penguins from penetrating the Senators' defensive structure enough to generate more than 26 shots on goal and make goaltender Craig Anderson's life miserable.

Another playoff game, more missing offense. The Penguins have now scored two or fewer goals in seven of their past eight.

"Flower has carried us here," Cullen said. "He's played so well for us. That makes it even worse that we kind of hung him out to dry. Bottom line is we didn't play well. We have to figure it out here as a group. We have to understand that it's not going to be easy. We have to put our best effort out there. We have to win battles. We have to fight a little bit. We didn't tonight."

Four of the Penguins' top-six forwards have struggled to score of late.

Sidney Crosby's third period goal snapped a seven-game goal-less stretch for him. An encouraging sign but not enough. Conor Sheary hasn't scored in 14, Chris Kunitz 10 and Jake Guentzel four. Hardly ideal production from four of your top six forwards.

Shots on goal have been a problem, too.

Crosby had 10 shots on goal in his last seven games before Game 3. Sheary had one or none in eight of his 13 playoff games before Game 3. Olli Maatta (13 shots on goal) had been more of an offensive threat than Guentzel (eight) and Nick Bonino (10) over the previous seven games.

Doesn't matter who, though. The Penguins, a puck-possession team under coach Mike Sullivan

Senators center Kyle Turris scores on Matt Murray in the Penguins' Game 3 loss. (Peter Diana/Post-Gazette)

and the regular season shots on goal leaders, have to do better here.

"You have to work for those extra breaks," Kunitz said. "You have to be putting a higher quantity of shots at their goalie and making it tougher for their goalie to see. It's not enough to have shots from the outside and no one in front finding those rebounds. Craig Anderson is playing well. He's seeing the puck well. We have to make it tough on their goalie if we're going to have a chance in this series."

Bottom-six production has lacked, too. Cullen doesn't have a point in six games. Bonino has gone without a goal in nine. Until Crosby's goal, the power play had been bad as well, his nifty stick play in front snapping a two-for-25 funk for that unit.

"We're not scoring goals right now," Cullen said. "It's important for us to do that if we want to win. I don't think we battled hard enough at either end of the ice to expect to score goals and expect to win a game."

You could blame injuries for the loss. No Kris Letang or Justin Schultz. Neither Brian Dumoulin nor Trevor Daley are fully healthy. The Penguins were without Bryan Rust, Schultz and Patric Hornqvist on this night.

But nobody around the Penguins will blame injuries.

They will, however, blame a lousy start. Odd bounces, sure, but the Penguins were hardly ready from the drop of the puck.

"When you give a goal that early in the game, against a team that's playing at home, it gives their team a lot of energy," Sullivan said, speaking of Mike Hoffman's tally 48 seconds in. "We have to be ready right from the drop of the puck. We have to be better.

"You can't lose a first period by four goals and think you're going to win."

Marc Methot made it 2-0 at 10:34 off another odd bounce. He pinched at the left point, fired a shot off Fleury's shoulder that later hit Ian Cole's skate or shin pad before going in.

Derick Brassard stretched the Senators lead to 3-0 at 12:28 of the first when he slipped behind Mark Streit, playing his first game since April 9, and picked up a gorgeous backdoor pass from Clarke MacArthur.

Zack Smith's wraparound goal at 12:52 of the opening period meant a 4-0 lead and curtains for Fleury, who allowed four goals on nine shots.

The situation was as devastating as it was surprising; in his last five playoff starts at Ottawa, Fleury went 5-0 with a 2.13 goals-against average and a .920 save percentage.

By the time Matt Murray allowed a goal to Kyle Turris at 18:18 of the third period, this one was long over. Crosby's power-play goal at 6:07 did little to change that.

"There's only one way to go," Cullen said. "We have a group that's been there. We've done it. We have to decide the way we want to play. If we play the right way, we give ourselves a really good shot. If we don't, this is what happens. We know that. There's no reason for that." ▪

Matt Murray makes a save against the Senators. He took over for Marc-Andre Fleury after Fleury allowed four goals on nine shots. (Peter Diana/Post-Gazette)

Eastern Conference Final, Game 4

MAY 19, 2017 · OTTAWA, ONTARIO
PENGUINS 3, SENATORS 2

A Change of Fortunes

Murray Makes Most of 1st Playoff Start This Year

By Jason Mackey

Matt Murray was well-aware of the situation. Down, 2-1, in the Eastern Conference final. On the road. The threat of some serious doom and an elimination game looming.

All of that mattered, of course.

Just not as much as one simple, little thing: Murray didn't want to let his coach down.

Mike Sullivan made a decision Friday — actually Thursday evening when he apparently texted Murray — that was met with some skepticism from outside the organization, starting Murray and sitting Marc-Andre Fleury for Game 4 against the Senators.

But Murray made his coach look awfully smart by stopping 24 of 26 shots in a 3-2 win. It turned out to be the spark the Penguins needed.

"It's always a big boost when your coach has the confidence in you to play a game like this, especially after so long," said Murray, who hadn't started a game since April 6. "I really appreciated the confidence that he put in me. I really tried to

put my best game on the ice and pay him back for his decision. I tried to do my best to give the team a chance to win."

Although he was touched for two goals, Murray mostly looked like the goaltender who backstopped the Penguins to a Stanley Cup last season and won 32 games in the regular season in 2016-17.

His rebound control was especially good early, with pucks sticking to him. Other times, Murray strategically funneled shots to the outside. Never was he flipping or flopping or giving anyone reason to be concerned.

"It's not an easy thing to do, but all you can do is jump in and try not to think about it," Murray said. "Just go with the flow of the game and let yourself get lost in the game a little bit. I thought I did a pretty good job of that."

As a result of the win Friday night, the Penguins improved to 12-2 in the playoffs under Sullivan after a loss.

With Ottawa buzzing as a result of a goal late

Penguins head coach Mike Sullivan gives referee Kevin Pollock an earful after a no-call against the Senators in Game 4. (Peter Diana/Post-Gazette)

in the second period, Murray made three keys stops in a 17-second stretch early in the third on Mike Hoffman, Erik Karlsson and Tom Pyatt.

Held to two or fewer goals in six consecutive games and in seven of their past eight, the Penguins got goals from Olli Maatta, Sidney Crosby and Brian Dumoulin.

They hadn't reached the three-goal mark since Game 2 of the Eastern Conference semifinals against Washington, but they turned in their most aggressive performance so far in this series, finishing with 35 shots on goal.

"As a whole each line generated some good chances," Crosby said. "We played the right way. We were physical. We were on our toes a bit more. Got the result we wanted."

That was one of the takeaways from this one, but it was hardly the only one.

How about where the Penguins shots came from? Sullivan and his players have talked about the need to generate offense from closer to Ottawa goaltender Craig Anderson. Eight of the Penguins' first 12 shots on goal came from below the dots.

Crosby's power-play goal on Anderson's doorstep gave the Penguins a 2-0 lead and was the perfect picture of this approach.

"As I've said all along here, this group has a knack for responding the right way to any of the adversities or the challenges that this team has been faced with," Sullivan said. "I think it always starts with our leadership. It starts with our captain. I think he leads by example, and I thought he had one of his best games [Friday]."

The Penguins have also been searching for secondary scoring. Crosby, Malkin, Phil Kessel and Jake Guentzel had more goals (26) than the rest of the Penguins combined (18) entering this one.

Which is why Maatta pinching and sneaking

a shot under Anderson's arm as he did to kick off the scoring should be seen as important. Or Dumoulin's point shot glancing off Dion Phaneuf's skate later. Offense from different sources.

"Just getting a goal was nice," Maatta said of his first-ever playoff game. "It's really exciting to score goals on a big stage like this. At the same time, I think we played a great game today. We started out well. Third period, they made a push. We did a good job pushing back."

Need more takeaways? Those 35 shots on goal were the Penguins' second-most of the postseason and the first time they had 30 or more since Game 3 of the Eastern Conference semifinals.

Another encouraging sign for the penalty kill, which snuffed out four Ottawa power plays — the Senators are 0 for 25 over the last nine games — to make it now 13 in a row and 22 of the last 23 killed against the Senators.

One of the few negative storylines going forward could be the loss of Chad Ruhwedel in the final minute of the period. He suffered a concussion, forcing the Penguins to yet again finish with five defensemen.

"Any time a defenseman goes down, it seems like we come together," Dumoulin said. "It seems like the forwards make that extra effort to come back and get the line and make it easier for us to change. I mean, it's not easy playing with five defensemen, but we've done it before. I think we did a good job of keeping our shifts short and just trying to get pucks out and keep the game simple."

Murray has a knack for keeping things simple and playing a quiet, positionally sound game. It's one of the reasons he got this assignment, and it was evident early on.

Although Murray said his game waned a little late, it's tough to give him too many bad marks. The

Sidney Crosby scores against Senators goalie Craig Anderson in the second period of the Penguins' 3-2 win. (Peter Diana/Post-Gazette)

goals he did allow were actually fairly reasonable.

On the Senators' first goal, Ryan completed a gorgeous feed from a distance, and Clarke MacArthur finished from the slot.

A double deflection led to the Senators second tally, a puck that caromed off Tom Pyatt's skate at 14:59 of the third period.

"I just tried to approach it like any other game," Murray said. "I had to come back from injury before this year. Basically try not to think about it. Just kind of jump in, just play. That was my focus.

"The team made it a pretty easy game for me. They did a really good job. They blocked a lot of shots, especially late. Really good overall team effort." ∎

MAY 21, 2017 · PITTSBURGH, PENNSYLVANIA
PENGUINS 7, SENATORS 0

Lesson in Taking Control

Offensive Output Puts Penguins on Edge of Cup Final

By Jason Mackey

Hockey's best offensive team had been unable to score goals. Like Aroldis Chapman losing his fastball or Usain Bolt running the 40-yard dash in 5 seconds flat. Scoring is what these Penguins do. Only they hadn't done it for the better part of three weeks.

Until Game 5.

The Penguins offense is apparently alive and well, and it bopped the Ottawa Senators over the head more than a few times throughout a 7-0 thrashing in Game 5 of the Eastern Conference final at PPG Paints Arena, one that wasn't even as close as the score might indicate.

"We found our game," Evgeni Malkin said. "We haven't scored a lot [the first four games of the series]. We saved it for this game. Everything worked. Good day for us."

Now, the clicking-on-all-cylinders Penguins hold a 3-2 series lead with a chance to close it out in Game 6 at Canadian Tire Centre, the organization's sixth trip to a Stanley Cup final just one win away.

The seven-goal output — the high-water mark

for them this postseason — came after the Penguins went nine games scoring three or fewer goals, six in a row before Game 4 scoring one or two.

Weird for the team that led the NHL in regular-season goal-scoring and had been among the postseason leaders until its recent downturn.

"You're not going to score seven goals every game, but we had chances," said Olli Maatta, who kicked off the scoring with his second goal in as many games.

"They don't always go in, but [Sunday] they did."

How the Penguins got those chances — and staggered back to their feet after the equivalent of a seven-count — might turn out to be the story of the series. Or potentially the entire postseason.

Before Game 4 in Ottawa, with the Penguins coming off a putrid performance, coach Mike Sullivan juggled his lines. And in typical Sullivan style, there was a clear direction, a definitive purpose to what he was doing.

Sullivan used Chris Kunitz, Scott Wilson, Carter Rowney and Josh Archibald as guys who can essentially do some of the dirty work, blue-collar types, worker bees, spread from the first

Penguins Carter Rowney (37) and Nick Bonino (13) celebrate a goal by Scott Wilson (not pictured) on Senators goaltender Craig Anderson in the first period of the Game 5 blowout. (Matt Freed/Post-Gazette)

through the fourth lines.

Their presence would be used to force puck battles, and all four lines were coupled with speed elements in Jake Guentzel, Phil Kessel, Bryan Rust (replacing Conor Sheary for Game 5) and Carl Hagelin.

"We like to have a north-south guy on every line that helps us play the game we want to play," Sullivan said.

So the Penguins played the game they want to play in Games 4 and 5. They won battles. They used their speed. They shot. They played low in the zone, working the puck with their defensemen.

It was their game, and stylistically it provided a gigantic departure from what happened in Games 1-3, when the Penguins played entirely too much like the Senators for anyone's comfort level.

Just consider these numbers from the past two games, numbers that explain the shift that has occurred:

- The Penguins have scored 10 goals, with four of them coming via defensemen.

- They've tossed 71 shots at Senators goaltender Craig Anderson, who was forced into a game of musical chairs Sunday with Mike Condon.

- Five of their seven goals came from 13 feet or closer.

For three games, the Penguins shot 3-pointers. Now, they're driving the lane. But it's not just that.

A rare, humorous moment came about in Sullivan's postgame news conference when he was asked whether his star players have had to adjust to Ottawa's 1-3-1 defensive structure and the fact that they've had to now create offense in a different way.

How, essentially, that not as much of it can come off the rush.

"Yes," Sullivan said with a smirk, drawing laughs. "We have a group of players who instinctively want to play with the puck. That's what separates them from others. They're elite players, so sometimes these guys want to make plays when there isn't any ice to play on or there isn't a play to be made. So that's a discipline that I think this team has developed or we have to continue to work at so that we don't feed our opponent's counter-attack game or their transition game.

"We talk a lot about not beating ourselves and defining what that means. One of the easiest ways to defeat yourself is if you're careless with the decisions you make with the puck in the critical areas of the rink. Our team in particular has that challenge because of the DNA of this group. It is a strength of our team, but if we're not diligent, it can become a weakness of our team. That's something that we talk about with these guys daily."

Translated: The Penguins have had to change the way they attack. It took awhile, but they've finally figured it out.

"We know they're a better team," Ottawa coach Guy Boucher said. "Everybody knows that on the planet. They're the Stanley Cup champions. They're the best team in the league. That's no secret.

"We know to beat that team, we need to be at our very, very best. And we were not."

That scoring depth was evident in the fact that seven players contributed goals, and 11 had at least a point. Rust, Rowney and Archibald infused youthful energy; Malkin was flat-out dazzling with a few of the passes he made.

All four lines got goals. The power play scored three times. The penalty-kill threw up a fifth consecutive clean sheet, although Ottawa might want to start declining penalties the way that unit has gone (0 for 29 the past 10 games).

The Penguins did all this by accumulating an absurd amount of possession time, the same thing this group did last season. On Rust's goal, which

Sidney Crosby scores on Senators goaltender Craig Anderson in the big Game 5 win. Crosby also added an assist on the night. (Matt Freed/Post-Gazette)

deflected off his thigh, the Penguins had the puck in the offensive zone for 1:22 before it he scored.

"We just want to continue to throw pucks at the net, get guys there for second opportunities, too," Sidney Crosby said. "We've been doing that the past couple games, and [Sunday] we got rewarded for it."

The same day, of course, that they became the Penguins again.

"To have the effort that we had tonight," Sullivan started out, "the readiness and will to win that we've had conversations about over the last few weeks that is so important to win at this time of year ... when we play the type of game that we played [Sunday], it allows us to dictate the terms out there a little bit and play to the identity of this Penguins team." ■

MAY 23, 2017 · OTTAWA, ONTARIO
SENATORS 2, PENGUINS 1

Here Comes Game 7

Anderson Stops 45 Shots to Stall Penguins Push
By Jason Mackey

If any NHL team should be able to process the impact that a superb goaltending performance can have on a playoff game, it's the Penguins.

Whether it's been Marc-Andre Fleury or Matt Murray, the Penguins have gotten both.

On Tuesday, with a chance to close out the Eastern Conference final against the Ottawa Senators in Game 6, the tables were turned.

The Penguins mostly played the way they wanted to, checking pretty much every box except for beating Craig Anderson more than once. As a result, they suffered a 2-1 loss at Canadian Tire Centre that sends this series back to a Game 7 in Pittsburgh.

"I thought we were pretty good [Tuesday]," Trevor Daley said. "We didn't get the bounces that we probably deserved tonight. That's hockey. That's the way it goes. There was a couple nights that happened to us, and it went the other way. It is what it is. If we do a lot the same at home, we'll be fine."

The Penguins threw 46 shots on goal at Anderson. Only one from Evgeni Malkin beat him. The Penguins also had a 75-46 edge in attempted shots, an indication of how much they dominated possession.

The only hiccups were a five-on-three power-play goal for the Senators, the Penguins' inability to do anything on their own power play and the fact that Matt Murray was screened on the Senators' second goal, a rocket of a shot from Mike Hoffman at 1:34 of the third period.

All in all, nothing to freak out over.

"I think we played the way we needed to, honestly," Murray said. "Credit to them. They played a solid, defensive game. At the same time, we were controlling the play for the most part. Anderson had a big night. If not for him, it's a different result. We just keep our same focus. Worry about what we're doing. I think today we played the way we needed to."

Even the game-winning goal was a bit of a fluke. Or one where you tip your cap, although that isn't exactly Murray's style.

Mike Hoffman got it at 1:34 of the third period. Powerful shot from above the left circle.

Trevor Daley celebrates as the puck gets by Senators goaltender Craig Anderson in the second period of Game 6. The Senators challenged the goal and it was overturned. (Matt Freed/Post-Gazette)

Clank, clank and in.

Murray was screened on the play. Hoffman waits just long enough before unleashing a powerful shot.

"I'm not really one to tip my cap," Murray said. "He's a good shooter. He's one of the best shooters in the league. I just tried to be aggressive. I knew there wasn't a pass option. He did a really good job at holding it and waiting for that screen to get to the net. The guy in front, I think it might have been [Mark] Stone skated by right at the release point. I was late picking it up. He puts a pretty good shot post and in. That was a pretty good shot."

Some good news for the Penguins and their fans: Ottawa has never won a Game 7 in its history, going 0 for 5 when faced with that situation.

The Penguins, meanwhile, failed to close out a series on their first try for the third time these playoffs and fifth consecutive time overall.

Now, they face the challenge of trying to win their third consecutive Game 7 and second during this postseason run.

"We know how to play in these types of games," Bryan Rust said. "We're going to be at home in front of our fans. That's going to give us a bit of a boost. We're going to come out with a lot of energy."

A disallowed goal loomed large in this one.

At 3:04 of the second, Daley pushed a puck through in a scrum. Ottawa coach Guy Boucher argued for goaltender interference.

The easiest way to explain the reversal is this: Daley kept pushing Anderson while the puck was away, preventing him from making the save.

Or at least that's how those reviewing the call interpreted it.

"I didn't agree with it," Matt Cullen said. "Those are 50/50s nowadays. It's hard to know exactly where those stand. I don't know if anybody is 100-percent sure which direction those are going to go. It's the breaks of the game. We always handle the adversity really well. I thought again tonight we did. We responded. We played well. We just weren't able to finish it."

Malkin put the Penguins ahead, 1-0, at 4:51. He curled out to the bottom of the right circle, with Ottawa's Zach Smith trailing him. Anderson stopped Malkin's initial shot, but Malkin backhanded the rebound to complete a fantastic individual effort.

A bad turnover from Olli Maatta nearly resulted in the Senators tying the score, but Bobby Ryan misfired on a pass to Derick Brassard.

Ryan would atone for the gaffe, however, when he tied the score at 13:15 of the second.

The Penguins were down a pair of defensemen when Ron Hainsey went off for interference and Ian Cole picked up two minutes for high-sticking just 36 seconds later.

Without their two best penalty-killing defensemen, the Penguins gave up a power-play goal for the first time this series, Ryan blasting a one-timer from Kyle Turris from the right circle.

That snapped an 0-for-29 skid for Ottawa's power play, which hadn't scored since April 27. Their first power-play goal in 11 games snapped a scoreless stretch of 98:16.

The Penguins generated a ton of offense. Malkin produced seven shots on goal and Sidney Crosby six, including a pair of backhand attempts. In the second period alone, the Penguins registered 23 shots on goal to 10 for the Senators.

Crosby was also a consistent presence around the goal mouth, another good sign. Two that weren't: Stone elbowing him in the head and Kyle Turris tackling him, evidence of how much attention the Senators paid to Crosby.

Senators goaltender Craig Anderson dives for a loose puck in front of Jake Guentzel during a standout performance by the goalie in Ottawa's win. (Matt Freed/Post-Gazette)

"We generated a lot of good chances," Crosby said. "You got to convert on those. But the chances were there. If we bring that same effort in Game 7, we'll give ourselves a good chance."

After three games, there was not a good feeling after a Penguins loss in this building.

Way different in Game 6.

A sense of what they've done the past two games: just keep playing the way they want and a belief that the dam will eventually break.

"We've been in this situation before," Daley added. "We're a confident team in here. We have a lot of veteran guys. We've been here before. We know what we need to do to get the job done in Game 7." ■

MAY 25, 2017 · PITTSBURGH, PENNSYLVANIA
PENGUINS 3, SENATORS 2, 2OT

A Shot and a Cheer

Kunitz Punches Ticket to Final in 2nd Overtime
By Jason Mackey

History will show that Chris Kunitz scored at 5:09 of the second overtime to give the Penguins a 3-2 win over the Ottawa Senators in Game 7 of the Eastern Conference final at PPG Paints Arena.

The schedule will show that the Penguins will host Nashville in Game 1 of the Stanley Cup final.

But as important as Kunitz's goal was, delivering a second consecutive trip to hockey's grandest stage and the sixth in franchise history, this win was about so much more than one goal or one win.

It was about a team that has been so resilient under coach Mike Sullivan again sticking with it, through overtime, through a pair of squandered leads, through the problems that Ottawa presented in Game 7 and all series, through injuries and through adversity.

"I give these players credit," Sullivan said. "They find ways to win."

Just think about what this win says on a team level:

- The Penguins had a wretched history at home in Game 7s, losing seven of 10.

- Ottawa had been 6-1 in overtime this postseason.

- The Penguins were playing a Senators team that, by nature of their defensive system, was a problem from the start of this thing.

What happened?

The Penguins got better and better. They changed. Sullivan made tweaks. Players responded. They scrapped the original game plan and came up with a new one.

"I'm proud of our group for the resilience that they showed throughout the course of this series," Sullivan said. "When we play a counter-attack team, they have numbers back and they force you to have to chip pucks in. I think it challenges our group.

"It takes a certain discipline on our part to make sure that we manage the puck the right way between the blue lines. I think this series tested our group in that regard. I couldn't be more proud of our group for sticking with it."

If that sounds like a familiar refrain, it's probably because many of the night's stars did the same exact thing.

Chris Kunitz (middle) scores the game-winner in double OT against the Senators to win the series and advance to the Stanley Cup final. (Peter Diana/Post-Gazette)

Kunitz hadn't scored since Feb. 16 but produced two goals and an assist, his screen on Justin Schultz's third-period power-play goal making a gigantic difference.

Even this season has been a difficult one for Kunitz. He's had to embrace a fourth line role, kill penalties and fight through what turned out to be the worst offensive regular season of his career.

Schultz had missed the past four games with an upper-body injury and took several big hits. He still managed to score a huge goal and play 24:16.

Or what about Olli Maatta? The kid who was out of the lineup late in the regular season following hand surgery, the one who might not make the playoff lineup, the same guy who's been their best defenseman these playoffs.

All he did was play 31:57, deliver two hits and block three shots.

Their contributions now have the Penguins back in the Stanley Cup final for the second consecutive year, the first since Pittsburgh and Detroit did it in 2008-09.

"Now the fun begins," Maatta said, a smile plastered on his face. "It's going to be awesome."

There was also Conor Sheary, a healthy scratch the past two games who used that wakeup game to turn in his postseason performance and reclaim a spot next to Sidney Crosby.

And Ron Hainsey, in the playoffs for the first time in his career, loving everything but actually talking about that and logging 30:41 with four hits.

Or Matt Murray, who felt a pop before Game 1 against Columbus and had to think his Penguins playoff career went poof, at least for this season, only to get his job back this series and put a chokehold on it.

Now, Murray has a chance to win two Stanley Cups in technically one NHL season; he is still a rookie, after all.

But don't expect that group to get that far ahead of itself. That's probably why they've gotten this far in the first place.

"This is what you work hard for all year, to give yourself a chance," Sidney Crosby said. "In this situation, it's not something that happens very often. It's a great opportunity for us."

And work the Penguins did against the Senators. They poured it on in the first overtime period, registering eight of 10 shots on goal.

Phil Kessel had a gorgeous chance early in the first session but missed the net. Kunitz nearly ended it by batting a puck out of the air.

You had Kessel again with the puck going up and over Anderson and a two-on-one with Carter Rowney and Bryan Rust.

"We stuck with it," Crosby said. "We had a ton of chances."

Of course they did.

The same as they stuck with it when Kris Letang was lost for the year, and they were beaten over the head with the idea that they couldn't reach the Cup Final, let alone win it, without a world-class defenseman.

Or that the ship would eventually sink with all the second-half injuries.

Not so.

Especially not in this seesaw affair, one that will go down as one of the best hockey games in franchise history.

One played by one of the most resilient teams in franchise history, too.

"It shows a lot of mental fortitude," Ian Cole said. "For us to get right back on our game, keep plowing away, keep creating in the offensive zone and keep playing good defensively. Shows how mentally tough this hockey team is. We're very proud of that." ■

Phil Kessel can't find the net on a breakaway against Senators goaltender Craig Anderson in the first overtime of the Game 7 victory. (Matt Freed/Post-Gazette)